PRAISE FOR *LEADERSHIP TYPES*

"Laura Barnard doesn't just offer theories; she equips you with the tools to craft a distinct leadership style that can stand the test of time and adapt to the ever-changing demands of the professional world."

—**Dorie Clark,** *Wall Street Journal* **bestselling author of** *The Long Game* **and executive education faculty at Columbia Business School**

"Leadership is changing. The sound. The smell. The taste. The look. The FEEL. The modern leader is deeply authentic, dynamic, and fundamentally self-aware. Transformational leaders know how to create a shared vision and uniquely inspire each person to reach for it and past it. Laura Barnard is the perfect individual to usher in the modern leader and build them for excellence."

—**Joanna Lohman, author of** *Raising Tomorrow's Champions* **and former Washington Spirit and US Women's National Soccer Team Member**

"By embracing diverse leadership styles, individuals can leverage their strengths to gain a competitive edge in the corporate landscape and contribute to broader economic empowerment."

—**Sallie Krawcheck, CEO and founder of Ellevest**

"Laura Barnard's *LEADERSHIP TYPES* is more than just a book; it is a transformative experience that redefines the essence of leadership in the contemporary world and shatters outdated stereotypes. The clear, well-structured layout and seamless flow makes it an easy and insightful read. By weaving the rich and inspirational stories of diverse leadership examples throughout the text to bring to life the leadership types, Barnard invites readers to discover their unique leadership styles authentically, and opens a world of possibilities for leaders to embrace a richer,

more diverse array of leadership qualities. This is a valuable resource for anyone committed to leading with authenticity and impact."
— **Sofia B. Pertuz, PhD, managing director of inclusion and leadership development at Billie Jean King Enterprises**

"Leaders who adopt this framework are poised to not only enhance their own effectiveness but to drive meaningful and lasting change within their teams and the broader organization."
— **Frances Frei, professor at Harvard Business School and coauthor of** *Move Fast and Fix Things* **and** *Unleashed*

"Whether you are an experienced leader or just starting out, Barnard's insights are both profound and practical, ensuring that readers of all levels can understand and apply her innovative concepts. Her engaging narrative weaves together research, stories, and strategies that challenge the reader to think differently about leadership. It's a book that will stay with you, offering wisdom that can be revisited time and time again as you continue to grow and evolve in your leadership journey."
— **Neil B. Niman, PhD, founding director of Business in Practice Program and associate professor at the University of New Hampshire**

"Captivating, compelling, innovative and novel, inspiring and empowering! Laura Barnard's *LEADERSHIP TYPES* is a timely and transformative read that challenges traditional stereotypes and reframes leadership styles. Insights explored and shared in this book celebrate diversity and amplify untapped potential. This is a must-read for those aspiring to lead authentically and uniquely in a rapidly evolving world."
— **Dr. La Quita Frederick, former director and associate professor of the practice for the Sports Industry Management, Masters of Professional Studies program at Georgetown University**

"Barnard's stated intention is to crack open stagnant stereotypes of leadership, and contribute to the current questioning, and reimagining, of dominant organizational norms that routinely and harmfully limit entire groups of people. She introduces the SLE as an approach to help us 'stand out' instead of 'fit in.' I encourage anyone committed to substantial social change to internalize the book's powerful premise that each of us can discover our own authentic and unique core of power, and from that empowering place, engage in transforming our world."

—Dorie Blesoff, Adjunct Professor at Northwestern University School of Education and Social Policy

"Barnard's groundbreaking book is a testament to the power of authenticity in leadership and is an essential resource for anyone who wants personal and practical insights to embark on a path of transformation to enhance their leadership impact."

—Laela Sturdy, managing partner of CapitalG

"Laura Barnard has written a transformative guide on modern leadership, brilliantly explaining how dynamic and authentic leadership styles can foster innovation and creativity. This book is not only a guide but also as a catalyst for transformation, offering actionable insights essential for anyone looking to make a significant impact in their field. Laura's refreshing approach makes this book an indispensable tool for aspiring leaders in today's fast-paced world."

—Charles Inokon, cofounder and CEO of Cadence Cash

"Laura Barnard's *LEADERSHIP TYPES* is coming at such a critical moment when we need to throw out outdated ideas of leadership and instead, embrace models that better exemplify what dynamic and inclusive leadership looks like. This book not only offers an innovative framework for redefining what it means to be a leader, it also offers practical tools to help any person embody their own authentic leadership style."

—Camira Powell, vice president of brand purpose at Edelman

"An essential read to uncover your authentic leadership style."

—Danielle Donehew, executive director of the Women's Basketball Coaches Association

"Laura Barnard's *LEADERSHIP TYPES* redefines what it means to lead in the modern world. With an incisive look into today's leadership landscape, Barnard's book is an essential read for those who seek to uncover their authentic leadership style and leave a lasting impact."

—Teddra Burgess, managing director, federal civilian for Google Public Sector

"This book isn't just about *understanding* leadership. It's about fundamentally *questioning* what leadership has meant—and radically *shifting* what it will mean, going forward. Less talk. More action. All day. So, read this, grab your hype women and dismantle the damn patriarchy. LFG."

—Erin Gallagher, CEO and founder of Ella and creator of the #HypeWomen Movement

"*LEADERSHIP TYPES* is a call to introspection and action for anyone wishing to make a positive impact through leadership, providing the necessary tools to carve out a space where your voice can not only be heard but can also inspire change and drive progress."

—Allison Feaster, vice president of team operations and organizational growth for the Boston Celtics

"Transitioning from the world of competitive sports to business, I've learned firsthand the importance of adaptive leadership. *LEADERSHIP TYPES* provides an indispensable guide for leveraging diverse leadership styles to excel in any arena over the course of your career."

—Angela Ruggiero, four-time Olympian, cofounder and chair of the board of Sports Innovation Lab

"Laura Barnard has crafted an indispensable resource for the leaders of today and tomorrow. She presents a clear, compelling, and (radical) argument that leadership is not a monolith but a mosaic of diverse styles and strengths. This book offers a comprehensive look at how we can lead, highlighting the importance of understanding ourselves in order to guide others effectively and create lasting impact."

—Corinne Milien, founder and CEO of WRK

"*LEADERSHIP TYPES* will help any organization, team, or individual unlock their power and potential. Full of 'ah-ha!' moments for leaders at any level who are seeking to reflect on their unique style and tap into that style to lead in ways that are effective and authentic. Other models and assessments can increase self-awareness while the Spectrum of Leadership Empowerment (SLE) will undoubtedly boost self-actualization."

—**Christine Leung, president of the Chicago International Charter School**

"By shattering outdated stereotypes . . . *LEADERSHIP TYPES* invites leaders to authentically connect and resonate with a newfound clarity. Going through the exercise myself, I was so gratified, validated, and encouraged to own my unique leadership style in a way that's really getting results for me, expanding my influence, income, and impact! *LEADERSHIP TYPES* brilliantly applies Laura Barnard's deep experience, expertise, and wisdom from the world of branding to us as humans."

—**Nell Derick Debevoise, speaker, coach, facilitator, and international bestselling author,** *Going First* **and the** *Purpose Party Playbook*

"*LEADERSHIP TYPES* challenges the outdated monolithic vision of leadership, offering instead a transformative framework that encourages individuals to discover their inner leader. Barnard expands the definition of leadership and equips aspiring leaders with the perspectives to refine their leadership style. A must-read for future leaders."

—**Melanie Scarlata, director of corporate relations for The University of Chicago Booth School of Business**

"In *LEADERSHIP TYPES*, author Laura Barnard challenges conventional leadership archetypes, offering a fresh perspective on leadership styles tailored for underrepresented voices. Drawing from real life examples and research, this book empowers readers to embrace their unique leadership potential. A must-read for anyone interested in leadership development and diversity in leadership."

—**Noemi Wierwille, chief learning officer for Teach for America**

"What is your leadership style? If you struggle to answer that question concisely with confidence and authority, then this is the book for you! It answers all of your questions and teaches you about you. An extraordinary read for all!"

—**Teena Piccione, global transformation and operations executive at Google**

"An insightful read for new and aspiring leaders, Barnard's book offers a compelling perspective on the importance of authentic leadership and identifying one's bespoke style to aid in professional growth and transformation. This guide serves as an ideal complement to other leadership indicators like DiSC and Myers Briggs, and offers the reader a more holistic view into leadership identity, while providing the necessary tools needed to explore, communicate and promote one's true leadership brand."

—**Natalie Vujko, PHR, SHRM-CP, strategic HR, talent development and inclusion consultant**

"Finally, a modern guide to developing truly transformative leaders! In *LEADERSHIP TYPES*, Barnard first offers the opportunity for readers to reflect on their own unique approach to leadership using the Spectrum of Leadership Empowerment and then illustrates how one can learn to effectively lead by embracing their own authentic style and strengths. Empowering on so many levels, this is a must-read for all aspiring leaders!"

—**Dr. Kimberly O'Brien, PhD, LICSW, founder and director of Unlimited Resilience**

"It's time to rewrite the playbook on leadership and expand the definition of 'acceptable' leadership markers. If organizations truly want to drive transformative change there must be a paradigm shift in the way leadership capabilities are defined and assessed. This book provides a model and framework for doing just that. Do you want to play the game or change the game? If you answered the latter, this book is a must-read."

—**Faith Eatman MPH, MBA, independent Healthcare DEI consultant**

"The SLE model helps emerging leaders understand how they fit into their work world, while helping current leaders 'see' how each person fits into the ecosystem and culture the organization seeks to build."

—**Dr. Jennifer Monti, MPH, MD, health technology innovator at Meta**

"*LEADERSHIP TYPES* is a modern and updated take on antiquated principles of leadership that are no longer relevant to today's emerging leaders. Based on experiences and research, this book speaks to the reader in a way where they feel seen. The first step towards effectively building your brand is understanding your Leadership Type and Laura Barnard guides the reader to both places."

—**Shimmy Gray-Miller, TV basketball analyst, 24-year basketball coaching veteran**

"Finally! A book that is a true guide for organizations on how they can bring EQUITY to leadership, by shedding light on different leadership styles, therefore making room for the many voices that have historically been overshadowed."

—**Deanna Barnes, senior director of inclusive partnerships at DoubleVerify, and author of** *A Very Good Helper*

"An innovative guide to help you navigate the complexities of leadership with insight, care, and practical wisdom."

—**Dr. Robin Vora, chair of ophthalmology, The Permanente Medical Group**

"*LEADERSHIP TYPES* is an empowering and accessible book that is data-informed, person-focused, and drives the reader to actively engage in leadership based on the widely applicable yet individualized approach of the unique SLE model. Laura Barnard's writing is vulnerable, inclusive, and authentic, encouraging the reader to engage in the larger responsibility of leadership, not only to learn more about oneself, but to apply that knowledge to improve the spaces we enter and to inspire others. This book artfully calls out stereotypes and demands the intentional dismantling of systems

that no longer serve us. It is a timely reminder of the need to rethink how we define leadership and identify and support diverse leaders. The compelling style and organization of the book, use of supportive visuals, and highlighting a variety of leaders as examples of each type set it apart as the most unique and practical book on leadership that I've ever read."
—**Tai Duncan Atteberry, vice president of corporate social responsibility for Crespo Labs**

LEADERSHIP TYPES

A Barrier-Breaking Approach to
Transform the Leadership Landscape

LEADERSHIP TYPES

A Barrier-Breaking Approach to Transform the Leadership Landscape

LAURA BARNARD

Copyright (C) 2024 Laura Barnard. All rights reserved.

No part of this publication shall be reproduced, transmitted, or sold in whole or in part in any form without prior written consent of the author, except as provided by the United States of America copyright law. Any unauthorized usage of the text without express written permission of the publisher is a violation of the author's copyright and is illegal and punishable by law. All trademarks and registered trademarks appearing in this guide are the property of their respective owners.

For permission requests, write to the publisher, addressed "Attention: Permissions Coordinator," at the address below.

PYP Publish Your Purpose

Publish Your Purpose
141 Weston Street, #155
Hartford, CT, 06141

The opinions expressed by the Author are not necessarily those held by Publish Your Purpose.

Ordering Information: Quantity sales and special discounts are available on quantity purchases by corporations, associations, and others. For details, contact the author at hello@leadershiptypes.com.

Edited by: Nancy Graham-Tillman, Lily Capstick
Cover design by: Nelly Murariu
Typeset by: Jet Launch

ISBN: 9798887971995 (hardcover)
ISBN: 9798887971988 (paperback)
ISBN: 9798887971971 (ebook)

Library of Congress Control Number: 2024906541

First edition, August 2024

The information contained within this book is strictly for informational purposes. The material may include information, products, or services by third parties. As such, the Author and Publisher do not assume responsibility or liability for any third-party material or opinions. The publisher is not responsible for websites (or their content) that are not owned by the publisher. Readers are advised to do their own due diligence when it comes to making decisions.

Publish Your Purpose is a hybrid publisher of non-fiction books. Our mission is to elevate the voices often excluded from traditional publishing. We intentionally seek out authors and storytellers with diverse backgrounds, life experiences, and unique perspectives to publish books that will make an impact in the world. Do you have a book idea you would like us to consider publishing? Please visit PublishYourPurpose.com for more information.

To my wife, Lindsay Gaskins, and our three daughters,
Lulu, Frannie, and Joanie,
for giving me the strength and confidence to be me
and help others do the same.

CONTENTS

Why I Wrote This Book and Why Now	1
Who This Book Is for and How It Is Structured	15
Breaking With Leadership Stereotypes	23
The Spectrum of Leadership Empowerment™ (SLE)	29
Meet The 12 Leadership Types	42
Quadrant 1: The Power to Create	44
Meet The Visionary	46
Meet The Legend	56
Meet The Innovator	66
Quadrant 2: The Power to Awaken	76
Meet The Trailblazer	78
Meet The Catalyst	88
Meet The Ignitor	100
Quadrant 3: The Power to Unite	110
Meet The Connector	112
Meet The Protector	122
Meet The Champion	132
Quadrant 4: The Power to Structure	144
Meet The Pathfinder	146
Meet The Navigator	156
Meet The Guide	166
Find Your Leadership Type	176
Take the Leadership Types Into Action	180
Acknowledgments	197
Bibliography	199
About the Author	201

A NOTE FROM THE AUTHOR

Dear Reader,

In this book, we have tried our best to integrate the most forward-thinking and expansive perspectives and language on leadership, gender, race, and identity. However, we recognize the ever-evolving nature of our world and these critical topics. As such, some of the insights, references, or examples shared in this book may become outdated or less relevant over time. While we are presenting what we believe to be an evergreen approach to unlocking the leadership potential within all of us, this book reflects a snapshot in time, and we humbly acknowledge the limitations inherent in capturing a complex subject matter in a dynamic landscape.

Additionally, we would like to express gratitude to all of our BREAKTHRU clients and collaborators, as well as the hidden figures whose stories we have highlighted. Thank you for informing our innovative and inclusive leadership development approach and enriching the content of this book.

WHY I WROTE THIS BOOK AND WHY NOW

The foundational premise of this book is that *everyone* has the capacity to be an effective leader, not just those who "fit the mold" of what we have historically come to expect leaders to look and act like. Each of us has a unique set of leadership characteristics and qualities—a "Leadership Type"—that can guide us to lead more authentically and better connect and communicate with others to maximize our impact.

When we understand, embrace, and celebrate a fuller spectrum of Leadership Types, we ensure that no talent or potential goes untapped. We open ourselves and others to greater possibilities for personal and professional growth. We unlock our greatest potential.

Leadership Types are unique to each of us, taking into account our internal motivations and external contexts. They help us reflect and give us a way to lean into what feels authentic, what sets us apart from others, and what makes us feel special. Identifying and understanding our Leadership Types gives us a way to step into our own power and break traditional leadership stereotypes that hold us back. Leadership Types can also help us shape and inform the personal **Leadership Brands** we want to share with the world.

Leadership Brands

Quick Definition:

A Leadership Brand is a strategic embodiment of leadership qualities and behaviors that aligns with both personal strengths and professional goals, enhancing a leader's ability to influence, drive change, inspire trust, and make an impact on individuals, teams, organizations, communities, and society.

Three Key Things to Know About This Topic:
- Developing a strong Leadership Brand helps leaders establish a recognized presence that aligns their authentic leadership style and values with their professional goals, increasing their influence and impact.
- A strong Leadership Brand helps guide a leader to communicate a clear vision and mission, and engage and motivate teams, which is essential for driving effective change and achieving organizational goals.
- By clearly articulating what makes them unique and their leadership philosophy, leaders can distinguish themselves in competitive environments, making them more attractive for advancement and additional leadership opportunities.

Why You Should Care About This Topic As a Leader:

Building your Leadership Brand is crucial because it not only enhances your professional visibility and influence but also significantly impacts your ability to lead effectively and authentically. A well-defined, consistent, and cohesive Leadership Brand ensures that your leadership style is honed, recognized and respected, facilitating better team alignment, increased stakeholder trust, and greater effectiveness in driving organizational initiatives.

To learn more about this topic,
visit leadershiptypes.com/resources/leadership-brands/
or scan QR code:

I am writing this book as the proud founder of BREAKTHRU Brands, an innovative leadership development solution focused on empowering underrepresented leaders. Our agency's expertise lies in strategically guiding leaders toward gaining greater clarity into their identities, growing confidence in their own competencies, and leading authentically and effectively through building powerful personal Leadership Brands. I am honored and privileged to be able to share the strategic insights our passionate team has uncovered through our work and share them with you through the pages of this book. We have seen what high-impact, high-achieving leadership can look like, and we want you to help us continue to change the face of leadership.

This book exists to help you uncover, articulate, and champion your unique Leadership Type and set you on the path toward building your unique brand of leadership, especially if you have been historically underrepresented. This book also exists to create a diversity, equity, and inclusion (**DEI**) paradigm shift: moving from creating spaces where everyone is merely included to creating spaces where everyone is powerfully represented and authentically *empowered*. Imagine a world in which your unique qualities are not just tolerated but celebrated. Where your voice is not just heard but amplified.

DEI

Quick Definition:

Diversity, Equity, and Inclusion (DEI) refers to policies and practices aimed at promoting a diverse workplace where all individuals are treated fairly, have equal access to opportunities, and feel included in all aspects of the organization. The backlash against DEI includes resistance or opposition to these initiatives, often stemming from misunderstandings, fear of change, or perceived threats to existing power structures.

Three Key Things to Know About This Topic:
- DEI enhances creativity, decision-making, and overall performance by incorporating a wider range of perspectives and skills.
- Backlash and resistance to DEI can take many forms, from passive non-compliance to active opposition, potentially derailing the benefits DEI brings to an organization.
- Effective leadership is critical in navigating and mitigating backlash against DEI, ensuring that DEI efforts are understood, embraced, and integrated into the organizational culture.

Why You Should Care About This Topic As a Leader:

As a leader, embracing and promoting DEI within your organization is crucial not only for fostering a positive workplace culture but also for enhancing business outcomes. Understanding and addressing the backlash against DEI initiatives is equally important, as it enables you to combat resistance effectively and uphold the integrity and success of your DEI efforts. By actively supporting DEI, you contribute to a more inclusive and equitable work environment that attracts and retains top talent, drives innovation, and aligns with ethical standards and societal expectations. Moreover, handling DEI backlash with informed and strategic responses reinforces your leadership role as an agent of positive change, ensuring that your organization remains resilient and competitive in a diverse global market.

To learn more about this topic,
visit leadershiptypes.com/resources/diversity-equity-inclusion/
or scan QR code:

Why does this matter and why now? Because we are in the midst of a generational shift. From a gender, ethnicity, racial, and identity perspective, the demographics of the US are shifting rapidly. Women now represent more than half of the college-educated labor force.[1] It is projected that by 2030, more people will be added to the population through net international migration than from natural increase, and by 2060, one in three Americans will be a race other than White.[2] Today, over 17 percent of adults younger than thirty identify as lesbian, gay, or bisexual compared to 8 percent of those ages thirty to forty-nine, 5 percent of those ages fifty to sixty-four, and 2 percent of those sixty-five and older.[3] Our country and the world are changing rapidly, and we need different tools, policies, procedures, and approaches to support and develop leaders for this modern time.

Now more than ever, the world needs your leadership, your vision, and your unique approach to solving problems and driving change. You have within you the raw materials to be not just a great leader but an extraordinary one. So the question is not whether you can become a great leader but whether you will seize the tools and insights needed to unleash that potential and turn that raw material into something profoundly impactful. *Your individuality as a leader is your strategic advantage.* And our strong belief at BREAKTHRU is that leaders and organizations who understand, embrace, and actively support this notion will thrive.

---

1. Richard Fry, "Women Now Outnumber Men in the US College-Educated Labor Force," Pew Research Center, September 26, 2022, https://www.pewresearch.org/short-reads/2022/09/26/women-now-outnumber-men-in-the-u-s-college-educated-labor-force/.
2. Jonathan Vespa, Lauren Medina, and David M. Armstrong, "Demographic Turning Points for the United States: Population Projections for 2020 to 2060," United States Census Bureau, last modified February 2020, https://www.census.gov/content/dam/Census/library/publications/2020/demo/p25-1144.pdf.
3. Rachel Minkin, "Diversity, Equity and Inclusion in the Workplace," Pew Research Center, May 17, 2023, https://www.pewresearch.org/social-trends/2023/05/17/diversity-equity-and-inclusion-in-the-workplace/.

I created this book as a tool to help you elevate your authentic leadership, empower you to rise within your organization, influence your industry, enhance representation in decision-making, and in turn make the world a more equitable place. May this book be an accelerant for your journey toward empowerment, confidence, clarity, and indelible impact.

I have devoted my professional career to better understanding and applying theories of psychology, branding, and leadership development to realize success and help those around me do the same. My insights are informed by my many experiences and studies. I have competed as a Division I athlete, studied psychology at Harvard, earned an MBA in strategic marketing and management from the University of Chicago Booth School of Business, spent nearly two decades leading global and iconic brands, and gained hands-on experience crafting personal Leadership Brands for thousands of high-impact business, sports, and nonprofit leaders through our work at BREAKTHRU. I hope this book gives you a fresh perspective on the impact of effective leadership and helps you realize your *own* definition of success.

While at Harvard, I was most impacted and inspired academically by my advisor and Professor of Social and Organizational Psychology, the late, great J. Richard Hackman, and personally by my basketball coach and leadership expert, the legendary Kathy Delaney-Smith. Since my days immersed in social psychology and team dynamics there, I have gravitated toward **positive psychology.** To bring out the best in ourselves and others, that approach helps us find ways to better understand why and how we think, feel, act, and behave in the ways that we do.

Positive Psychology

Quick Definition:

Positive psychology in leadership focuses on enhancing leaders' ability to foster an environment of well-being, resilience, and high performance by emphasizing the assets, strengths, and virtues that enable individuals and teams to thrive.

Three Key Things to Know About This Topic:
- Positive psychology empowers leaders to cultivate personal and team resilience, foster a positive work environment, and encourage innovative thinking.
- Integrating positive psychology into leadership practices promotes a workplace culture characterized by higher job satisfaction, greater creativity, and increased overall well-being.
- Leaders who apply positive psychology principles can significantly boost team performance and adaptability, leading to sustainable organizational success and competitive advantage.

Why You Should Care About This Topic As a Leader:

Understanding and applying positive psychology as a leader is crucial for developing a strong, motivated team capable of facing modern challenges with optimism and creativity. By fostering an environment that values well-being and psychological resilience, you not only enhance individual and team performance but also contribute to a more fulfilling and engaging workplace. This approach not only attracts and retains top talent but also aligns with broader organizational goals, driving success and innovation. As a leader, your commitment to positive psychology can transform the traditional workplace into a vibrant, supportive, and highly productive environment.

To learn more about this topic,
visit leadershiptypes.com/resources/positive-psychology/
or scan QR code:

When I graduated from Harvard, I eagerly (and rather obliviously) jumped into the thing I knew as "Corporate America" with two feet. This was what most of my classmates were doing and what I thought I was supposed to do to put my degree to work and have financial freedom. I joined one of the largest banks in the world, and the sky was the limit. Or so I thought.

When I learned about the existence of things like "management training programs" and "professional development" in the corporate world, I was like a kid in a candy store. (Yes, I am kind of a nerd.) I was excited to learn more about all these resources and wanted to proactively manage my career development. So year after year I completed assessments via Clifton StrengthsFinder, Hogan Assessments, and Myers-Briggs Type Indicator, as well as the DiSC personality test, 360-feedback sessions, and performance reviews. I pored over the results and reports, listened carefully to the feedback from my managers and human resources colleagues, worked on the competencies and developmental areas they suggested, and took on the projects necessary for me to climb the ladder. I again did what I was "supposed" to do without realizing that I was repeatedly being boxed in and limited by the very assessments and development tools designed to supposedly expand my horizons and aid in my development. I felt like I was constantly trying to fit in and being pressured to become someone I was not.

In my early twenties, I came out as a lesbian, first to my friends and family and then to my work colleagues. I remember being asked by my business school classmates at the time if I was "going to be out" in the recruiting and interviewing process with companies and thinking that the question was absurd. Of course I was going to be out. Why would being a lesbian be a hindrance to me in the recruiting process? I would not want to work for a company that does not value diversity and inclusion anyway.

While at the time I did not recognize overt **stereotyping, bias, and discrimination** in the workplace for being a woman or being gay, as I rose in the ranks I was told more than once by my various managers that I was not assertive or dominant enough to be a CEO or general manager, which was my ambition at the time. I was told that I was "too affable," "too nice," "not strong enough at driving an agenda," or "not assertive enough." And when I looked to the top of nearly every organization I worked for, I saw only White,[4] cisgendered, heterosexual men who displayed the traits I was lacking. Though I was told that I was a good fit for the head of brand or marketing roles, I was also told that I had a lot of work to do to get to the highest levels within the organization. Executive coaches and additional resources were pushed toward me, but it felt like I would need to change who I was as a leader in order to rise up any further. My pathways to senior leadership roles seemed narrowed.

I remember at one point in a senior leadership meeting, where I was one of only two women at the table, I built up the courage to speak up about some noninclusive, bullying language that our CEO was using to describe a colleague. With a finger pointed in my face, and in front of all my peers, that CEO yelled at me, "You do not know *anything*!" Twice. In this painful moment, I realized that misogyny had always been there surrounding me. I was bumping my head on the glass ceiling, and my eyes were wide open to the leadership stereotypes and microaggressions constantly swirling around me and other members of historically marginalized groups within my organization. I started noticing increasingly more instances of both subtle and not so subtle bias and discrimination. Once I *really* saw all the inequities and the systems that were perpetuating them, I could not unsee them.

---

4. Ann Thúy Nguyễn and Maya Pendleton, "Recognizing Race in Language: Why We Capitalize 'Black' and 'White,'" Center for the Study of Social Policy, March 23, 2020, https://cssp.org/2020/03/recognizing-race-in-language-why-we-capitalize-black-and-white/.

Stereotypes, Bias, & Discrimination

Quick Definition:

Addressing stereotypes, bias, and discrimination in leadership involves understanding and actively combating the deep-rooted issues that limit diversity, foster inequality, and hinder organizational and societal progress. This requires leaders to recognize and rectify practices and cultures that perpetuate these biases, ensuring an equitable and inclusive work environment.

Three Key Things to Know About This Topic:
- Stereotypes and biases restrict the positive impact of diversity of leadership, reducing the variety of perspectives needed for innovation and effective decision-making.
- Biases are often ingrained in organizational cultures, influencing hiring, promotion, development, and daily interpersonal interactions, which can create toxic work environments and lower productivity.
- Leaders play a crucial role in shaping organizational culture; by addressing their own biases and setting clear anti-discrimination policies, they can foster a more inclusive and productive workplace.

Why You Should Care About This Topic As a Leader:

As a leader, actively addressing and dismantling biases, stereotypes, and discrimination not only improves your organization's performance but also sets a standard for ethical leadership. It contributes to creating a work environment where all employees feel valued and have equal opportunities to thrive. This commitment to equity and inclusion enhances employee satisfaction, attracts diverse talent, and boosts your company's reputation, aligning with modern ethical standards and societal expectations.

To learn more about this topic,
visit leadershiptypes.com/resources/stereotypes-bias-discrimination/ or scan QR code:

In 2019, I had enough of feeling boxed in, and I built up the courage to jump off the corporate ladder in the hope of regaining my identity as a leader and my sense of purpose. I did not know what I was going to do next or how exactly I was going to do it, but I knew I wanted to leverage my background, my experience, and my skill set to empower others to lead and to help change the face of leadership.

To be clear, traditional **leadership assessment tools**, such as the Myers-Briggs Type Indicator, are not nefarious or ineffectual. However, many of these tools are rooted in past patterns of leadership traits and behaviors and are leveraged to get individuals to fit into these patterns. As such, they perpetuate the status quo within organizations by limiting how we think about who can lead and how they "should" lead, thereby limiting our potential.

Leadership Assessment Tools

Quick Definition:

Leadership assessment tools are instruments used to evaluate and enhance leadership capabilities, providing insights into leadership styles, strengths, weaknesses, and areas for development. These tools have evolved from basic trait evaluations to complex frameworks that consider behavioral, situational, and inclusive aspects of leadership.

Three Key Things to Know About This Topic:

- Originally developed for military use, leadership assessment tools now apply across various sectors, adapting to the changing demands of leadership in diverse organizational contexts.
- Tools like the Myers-Briggs Type Indicator (MBTI), the DiSC assessment, CliftonStrengths, and 360-Degree Feedback provide different perspectives on leadership abilities and team dynamics, aiding in personal and organizational development.
- To remain relevant in today's diverse and dynamic work environments, these tools must evolve to capture a broader range of leadership styles and qualities, focusing on inclusivity, authenticity, and the unique paths of individual leaders.

Why You Should Care About This Topic As a Leader:

As a leader, embracing advanced leadership assessment tools is crucial for developing a deep understanding of your own leadership style and that of your team. These tools help identify areas for personal growth, enhance team dynamics, and foster a culture of continuous improvement. By adapting to more nuanced and inclusive assessment methods, you can better meet the needs of a diverse workforce and lead more effectively in a complex, rapidly changing world.

To learn more about this topic, visit leadershiptypes.com/resources/leadership-assessment-tools/ or scan QR code:

What if we could more fully recognize the spectrum of what leadership looks like? What if we had a more evolved methodology that encouraged people to be themselves and stand out rather than just fit in?

In this spirit, and to meet the needs of the cultural moment we are living in and equip the next generation of leaders to navigate and thrive, BREAKTHRU has created The Spectrum of Leadership Empowerment™ (SLE). The SLE provides common, positive language for understanding and valuing our individual differences, as well as practical insights that are easy to understand and put into practice, to make a difference in people's lives. It looks beyond the traditional, the obvious, and the established to seek out the hidden figures among us, recognizing, celebrating, and leveraging their diverse talents and the value they bring.

Our goal with the SLE is to inspire the vast reservoir of untapped potential within organizations, positioning it in a way that reshapes the future for the better. While diversity in the workplace has improved over time, there are still countless voices that go unheard, capabilities that go unrecognized, and leadership styles that go uncelebrated. Think about the hidden figures in your own life or community. They are the pioneers in the shadows, working tirelessly without the spotlight yet driving real change and impacting lives in ways big and small. To these unsung leaders, and to you who may feel overlooked or underrepresented, this book serves as a beacon of empowerment. Because we believe that leadership and empowerment should never be a privilege of the few.

As you turn these pages, I hope you feel seen, heard, and above all, empowered. I hope this book serves as a boost for you on your journey of self-discovery and growth, one that elevates your leadership to new heights, breaking stereotypes and smashing ceilings and barriers along the way. In taking the journey, I hope you do not just transform yourself; I hope you become a guiding light for transformation in your community and beyond.

This is not just another self-help book or leadership guide. This is your call to action. It is an invitation to break through traditional definitions and constraints and stand out rather than fit in, a summons to seek knowledge with a bold and unapologetic voice, and a directive to aspire toward a leadership identity that is uniquely and authentically your own. We all stand on the precipice of barrier-breaking change, and it is a leap we must dare to take. This is a rallying cry to all the hidden figures out there: Your time is now. Your leadership is needed, and this is your manual for empowerment.

Welcome to *Leadership Types: A Barrier-Breaking Approach to Transform the Leadership Landscape.*

WHO THIS BOOK IS FOR AND HOW IT IS STRUCTURED

If you are reading this book, you are a leader. Your leadership can take place *anywhere*, *anytime*, and among *anyone*; in formal settings or structures and informal groups or gatherings; among friends, families, colleagues, and communities; and inside and outside of organizations. The insights into your leadership that you will gain through reading this book will help you lead more effectively everywhere, **self-actualize**, realize your potential, and have a positive ripple effect on those around you, both personally and professionally.

Self-Actualization

Quick Definition:

Self-actualization in leadership is the process by which leaders strive to achieve their fullest potential, aligning their personal values with professional objectives to enhance their effectiveness and influence within an organization.

Three Key Things to Know About This Topic:
- Self-actualization helps leaders harness their full capabilities, fostering an environment of innovation and peak performance.
- By aligning personal values with professional actions, self-actualized leaders inspire trust and loyalty, enhancing team dynamics and organizational culture.
- Leaders who are self-actualized are better equipped to motivate their teams, navigate change, and effectively lead their organizations toward strategic goals.

Why You Should Care About This Topic As a Leader:

Leaders should seek self-actualization to not only improve their own performance but also to profoundly impact their organization. The process of striving for self-actualization not only cultivates a deeper level of self-awareness and personal mastery but also equips you to inspire and lead others more effectively. As you work towards your own self-actualization, you inherently create a more dynamic, innovative, and responsive leadership style that can significantly influence your team's engagement, cohesion, and productivity. Engaging in this continuous growth process ensures that you remain adaptable and resilient in the face of challenges, making you a more effective leader capable of driving meaningful change.

To learn more about this topic,
visit leadershiptypes.com/resources/self-actualization/
or scan QR code:

This book is for you if you are seeking to be empowered or are in a position to empower others. Perhaps you are an individual who is a member of an underrepresented group or a part of the nondominant culture within your organization and may have experienced or be experiencing feelings of insecurity and disconnection. You may feel like you are boxed in by others' evaluations or perceptions of you, are completely overlooked, or are not fully seen or heard in the workplace. You are not alone. In fact, most underrepresented leaders do not feel like they can be their authentic selves at work: "People in marginalized groups mask at work all the time to blend into the mainstream. If we tone down the parts of ourselves that are not represented in or experienced by the dominant group—whether it be a mental health condition, disability, sexual orientation, or gender expression—we minimize our chances of experiencing bias or alienation. In the workplace, masking occurs when one feels their identity will be disfavored in the environment they are in."[5]

When underrepresented leaders feel that they are not celebrated for who they are or that they are not truly seen and valued, they can experience a loss of confidence and perceived authority, which can further deter them from reaching their full potential. This book is not a panacea or a magic wand, but we hope it gives you concepts and language that make you feel like you not only fit in but are an integral, beautiful part of the leadership tapestry.

If you are a leader who is part of the dominant culture within an organization, we hope this book pushes you to think harder about your goals regarding advancing representation within your organization. Are you doing the bare minimum to promote an equitable work environment, or are you going above and beyond to lift up others who are not as advantaged or privileged as you? We hope you approach achieving these goals both personally and with intention.

---

5. Graci Harkema, "How to Bring Your Authentic Self to Work," Ascend, December 15, 2023, https://hbr.org/2023/12/how-to-bring-your-authentic-self-to-work.

Ultimately, this book is for you if you:

- ✔ want to lead more authentically and effectively;
- ✔ desire to feel seen, heard, and valued as a leader;
- ✔ are about to take on something new, such as a new role, founding a company, or starting a job search, and seek to know and speak about your leadership identity;
- ✔ want to reduce stereotypes, bias, or prejudice;
- ✔ are in a position to develop or support underrepresented leaders;
- ✔ believe that diversity, equity, and inclusion matter; and/or
- ✔ trust that there is potential to be unlocked in the teams and organizations that surround the leaders of today.

Before we dive into each of the Leadership Types and learn how to identify them, I want to share with you why and how these Types were developed, how they relate to one another, and how they all come together in the SLE.

The SLE is designed to inspire you to think *internally*, in terms of identifying and leaning into your **motivation** to lead, as well as *externally*, in terms of realizing and activating your full power as a leader. It was also designed to dismantle leadership stereotypes, help guide how you perceive yourself, and shift how others perceive you as a leader. This approach is intended to give you a way to explore your internal motivation and external power more deeply. Ultimately, the SLE shows leaders where their Leadership Type lands within the spectrum, illuminating a path toward achieving their greatest impact.

Motivation

Quick Definition:

Motivation in leadership refers to the dual role of a leader's personal drive and their ability to inspire and mobilize their team towards achieving common goals. It is the undercurrent that silently but profoundly influences leadership effectiveness, enhancing the ability to inspire, galvanize, and transform teams and organizations.

Three Key Things to Know About This Topic:

- Motivation is essential not only for maintaining a leader's personal drive but also for inspiring and motivating team members. It's about creating an environment where passion and dedication are contagious.
- A motivated leader can foster an organizational culture that values innovation, risk-taking, and proactive involvement, which are critical for navigating today's dynamic business landscape.
- By understanding and leveraging the intrinsic and extrinsic motivations of their team, leaders can enhance cohesion, job satisfaction, and organizational loyalty, positioning the team for long-term success.

Why You Should Care About This Topic As a Leader:

Understanding and harnessing motivation is critical for any leader aiming to achieve peak team performance and organizational resilience. By deeply engaging with what drives you and your team, you can create a more fulfilling, productive, and innovative work environment. This knowledge enables you to effectively inspire and lead your team through challenges, fostering an atmosphere of shared success and continuous growth.

To learn more about this topic,
visit leadershiptypes.com/resources/motivation/
or scan QR code:

The SLE is inspired by inclusivity and rooted in motivational psychology, meaning understanding what drives our thoughts, decisions, and actions. It consists of Leadership Types, our fresh take on the concept of **archetypes**, which are readily understood examples or models of people, behaviors, and personalities. This innovative approach is based on data and insights collected directly from interviews, observational studies, and collaborations with thousands of underrepresented leaders across industries through our work at BREAKTHRU. And as we continue to do our work, our conviction that there is much power in reshaping the future of leadership grows.

LEADERSHIP TYPES

Archetypes

Quick Definition:

Archetypes are universally inherent templates or symbols that shape human behavior, influence our perceptions, and resonate through culture, myths, and personal identities.

Three Key Things to Know About This Topic:
- Archetypes, as outlined by Carl Jung, a Swiss psychiatrist and psychoanalyst in the early 1900s, are foundational elements of the human psyche, shaping our experiences, emotions, and cultural narratives across time and geography.
- Understanding archetypes can significantly enhance leadership by improving communication, fostering empathy, and tailoring leadership strategies to align with the intrinsic motivations of teams.
- Contemporary research in psychology and neuroscience continues to explore the influence of archetypes, highlighting their relevance in therapy, personal development, and organizational dynamics.

Why You Should Care About This Topic As a Leader:

Understanding archetypes can transform your approach to leadership. By recognizing and utilizing the universal patterns that influence human behavior and motivations, leaders can craft compelling narratives, build stronger teams, and lead with greater empathy and effectiveness. This deeper insight allows leaders to connect profoundly with their teams, fostering an environment of shared values and unified purpose that drives organizational success.

To learn more about this topic,
visit leadershiptypes.com/resources/archetypes/
or scan QR code:

Innovative and inclusive, the SLE is a way to understand and think about diverse leadership styles, challenging stereotypes, and biases. Through this book, we invite you to explore and identify your own unique Leadership Type within the SLE and start on the path toward building your personal Leadership Brand. Our theory is that once an individual identifies their unique Leadership Type, they can leverage internal insights to begin to build their external brand—how they are experienced or perceived by others—more strategically as a leader. Leaders with strong personal Leadership Brands embodying salient Leadership Types can better relate to and communicate with others. They can also connect people, promote ideas and new ways of thinking, transform organizations, and create movements.

Before we dive into the design and intricacies of the SLE, I will explore one of the most significant barriers facing underrepresented leaders: leadership stereotypes. I will explain how the SLE was designed to help dismantle them, then introduce you to the 12 most salient Leadership Types comprising the SLE. Depending on your learning style or preference, you can read through the Leadership Types consecutively to explore the full spectrum of possibilities, or you can flip to the specific Leadership Type that you are most curious to learn more about based on your current context and specific goals.

At the end of the book, I provide you with implications for consideration and ideas about how to put the Leadership Types into action as an individual, team, or organization. I also invite you to chart your Type at LeadershipTypes.com. This quiz can help you quickly identify the Leadership Types that are most prominent in the way you lead today and provide insights into opportunities for unlocking your leadership power.

Collectively, we can begin to break down the leadership stereotypes that hold us back from realizing our fullest potential and shine a light on the untapped potential within us all.

BREAKING WITH LEADERSHIP STEREOTYPES

Leadership stereotypes root us in the past. They are persistent and pervasive headwinds that hold us back from unleashing the power of underrepresented leaders. Through our work and this book, BREAKTHRU is on a mission to dismantle these stereotypes by inspiring thinking and action that moves beyond stereotypical notions about leadership.

While there is no magic wand to eradicate something as deeply entrenched as stereotypes, within the SLE we are intentionally putting forward a model to help others understand, discuss, and develop leadership in a way that is more inclusive, empowering, and ultimately barrier-breaking, especially for leaders who historically have not been represented in leadership. In this way—working from the inside out—we are attempting to break down and dismantle stereotypes that exist in traditional **leadership development** methods and within organizations.

Leadership Development

Quick Definition:

Leadership development is an intentional effort to enhance the leadership capabilities of individuals or cohorts within organizations. It focuses on expanding leaders' ability to perform in roles that directly impact organizational success, integrating a blend of technical and soft skills such as strategic decision-making, emotional intelligence, and effective communication.

Three Key Things to Know About This Topic:
- Leadership development has evolved from an emphasis on innate qualities to recognizing the importance of cultivated skills and contextual awareness, reflecting changes in societal norms and organizational demands.
- Modern leadership development integrates psychological theories, technological advancements, and emphasizes the importance of diversity, equity, and inclusion, making it relevant in today's global and digital workplace.
- The ongoing evolution of leadership development practices is crucial to preparing leaders who are adaptable, inclusive, and capable of meeting the complex challenges of tomorrow's organizational landscapes.

Why You Should Care About This Topic As a Leader:

Engaging with leadership development is essential for any leader seeking to remain effective and relevant in an ever-changing global environment. Leadership development equips leaders with the necessary tools to handle dynamic organizational challenges, fosters a culture of continuous improvement, and ensures that leadership strategies are inclusive and adaptable. By investing in your leadership development and that of your team, you can drive innovation, enhance organizational resilience, and contribute to a more equitable and sustainable future.

To learn more about this topic,
visit leadershiptypes.com/resources/leadership-development/
or scan QR code:

From a definition-setting perspective, stereotypes are cognitive shortcuts that categorize people based on characteristics such as gender identity, orientation, ethnicity, race, or age. From these stereotypes, biases—generalized beliefs about groups of people based on prior assumptions—can form.

Because men have historically held (in the United States and many other countries) the vast majority of the positions of leadership and power, our society has developed deep-seated expectations about who should lead and what leadership behaviors should look like. According to an article from *Forbes*, "When people are asked about the stereotypical traits of leaders, they tend to talk about self-confidence, assertiveness, taking charge, solving problems, inspiring others, risk-taking, and action orientation—agentic qualities that are similar to the masculine stereotype."[6] Stereotypical leadership traits, as well as characteristics such as extraversion, tend to be rewarded, and organizations often more readily accept, understand, and promote individuals who display them. Traditionally that has been White, cisgender, heterosexual men in leadership roles, so they have served as the "standard" for leadership.

We have subsequently been conditioned to expect how leaders should look and act and have developed bias and prejudice about who is selected to lead and who is overlooked or left behind. Those who meet the expectations receive support and rise up. Those who do not get passed over or are forced out. Additionally—and unsurprisingly—most organizational leadership development programs and tools are designed with this traditional definition of what "strong leadership" looks like and how to support it, further reinforcing patriarchal structures and perpetuating leadership stereotypes.

Leadership stereotypes are deeply ingrained in our collective psyche, often operating beneath the surface of our awareness. They

---

6. Michael Milad, "Female Leadership: Overcoming Stereotypes about Choosing the Best Leader," *Forbes*, January 26, 2021, https://www.forbes.com/sites/forbescoachescouncil/2021/01/26/female-leadership-overcoming-stereotypes-about-choosing-the-best-leader/?sh=2f24e9051ccb.

are rooted in the past, steeped in a systemic history influenced by patriarchy, homophobia, and racism. These stereotypes, even when unacknowledged, continue to shape our perceptions and behaviors, perpetuating the status quo. They stifle individual leaders who are underrepresented, as well as organizations and companies, by causing them to overlook and thereby miss out on tapping into the leadership potential of diverse individuals. In this way, leadership stereotypes directly contribute to underrepresentation, most pervasively at the upper-middle and senior management levels of organizations. Not only is this underrepresentation inequitable, but it holds organizations back from reaching their full potential. It limits their pipeline of future talent and the perspectives that are represented in places where decisions are being made. And organizations, industries, and our broader society are missing out on people, ideas, and innovation that will drive progress.

White men have held the majority of the positions of power in the United States for generations, and this trend persists today: White, cisgendered men represent only around 30 percent of the US population, yet they represent around 60 percent of elected office positions and over 80 percent of Fortune 500 CEO seats.[7] When these White male leaders look around the room and the "leadership table," they hear and see themselves, and they get to decide who gets a seat at that table. We all become conditioned to what leadership looks like. And the longer that White men fill these seats, the longer these leadership stereotypes are perpetuated, making it harder to amend them.

We want to change that. We refuse to sit back and wait for someone else to decide who gets a seat and a voice at the table. The time is now. Change cannot wait.

While we have seen some progress in terms of policies, procedures, and practices around the recruitment, hiring, development,

---

7. Alexandra Villarreal, "White Male Minority Rule Pervades Politics across the US, Research Shows," *The Guardian*, May 26, 2021, https://www.theguardian.com/us-news/2021/may/26/white-male-minority-rule-us-politics-research.

and advancement of underrepresented leaders in the workplace over the last fifty years, according to a recent global report from the World Economic Forum, it will take more than 130 years until we reach gender parity.[8] And we are even further away from reaching parity based on race, orientation, ethnicity, or any other marginalized identity.

Time alone will not solve this underrepresentation. Action will. Equitable representation in leadership will not increase substantially without major changes in the culture, policies, and practices of the organizations where underrepresented leaders learn and work.

On our mission to advance gender, racial, and identity equity in leadership, BREAKTHRU aims to empower underrepresented leaders to stand up and speak out, to be seen and heard in a way that is authentic to them. We seek to give these underrepresented leaders a voice and a platform for organizational and societal change. In parallel to the higher-level policies and systemic changes required to close the **leadership gap**, we are taking a grassroots approach, focusing on individuals and their ability to drive organizational change. We want to change how we think and discuss what effective leadership looks like and who can and should lead.

---

8. Martin Armstrong, "It Will Take Another 136 Years to Close the Global Gender Gap," World Economic Forum, April 12, 2021, https://www.weforum.org/agenda/2021/04/136-years-is-the-estimated-journey-time-to-gender-equality/.

Leadership Gap

Quick Definition:

The leadership gap refers to the disparity between the demographic makeup of the leadership of an organization or group and the actual diverse composition of the community it serves. This gap highlights the underrepresentation of women, people of color, LGBTQIA+ individuals, and other marginalized groups in top leadership roles, impacting organizational and societal progress.

Three Key Things to Know About This Topic:
- Homogeneous leadership limits the range of ideas and experiences that are shared, stifling innovation and reducing the effectiveness of decision-making within organizations.
- The lack of diversity in leadership roles can demoralize employees and perpetuate harmful stereotypes, negatively impacting the self-esteem and career aspirations of individuals from underrepresented groups.
- Diverse leadership has been shown to increase organizational performance, with diverse companies experiencing better market responsiveness and competitive advantage.

Why You Should Care About This Topic As a Leader:

Diverse leadership drives innovation, mirrors the diversity of global markets, and enhances employee engagement and loyalty. By committing to closing the leadership gap, you foster a more inclusive, equitable, and dynamic organizational culture that attracts top talent and reflects the values of today's society.

To learn more about this topic,
visit leadershiptypes.com/resources/the-leadership-gap/
or scan QR code:

Together, we can increase inclusivity of opportunity in the boardroom, democratize access to the C-suite, and prioritize potential over pedigree. It is time to break down leadership stereotypes and redefine who gets a seat and a voice at the leadership table. It is time to stand out rather than fit in.

THE SPECTRUM OF LEADERSHIP EMPOWERMENT™ (SLE)

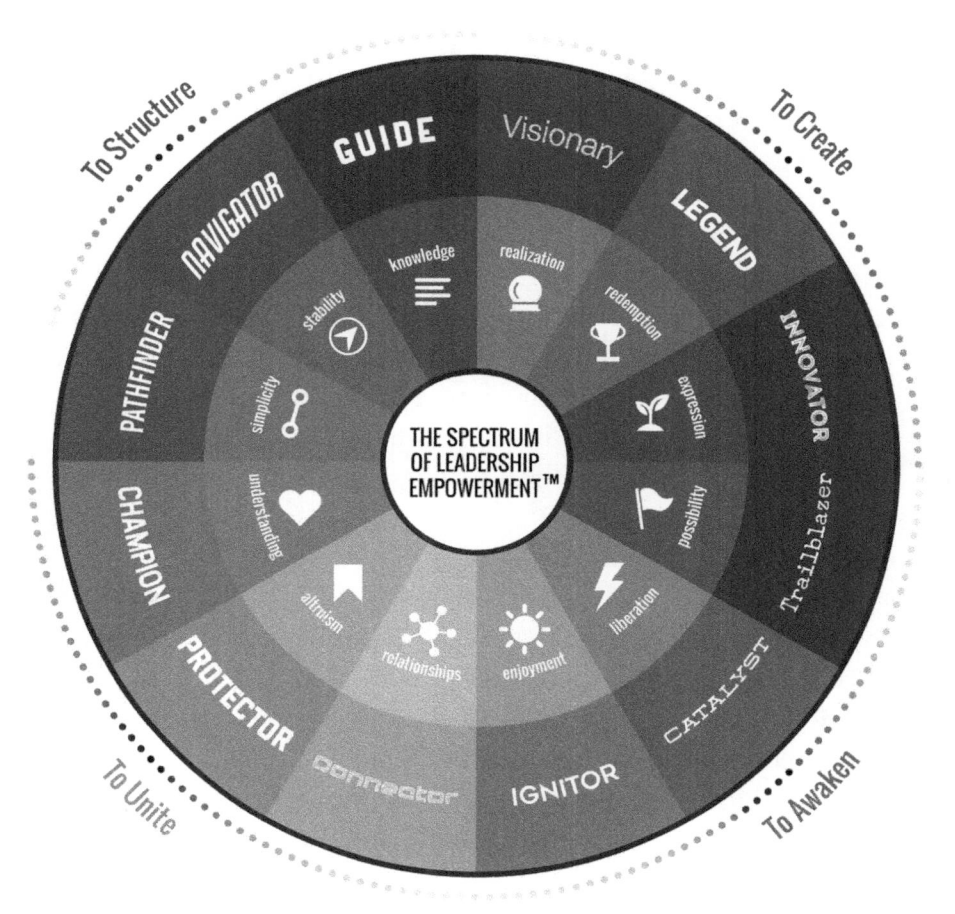

Our team at BREAKTHRU developed the SLE to inspire, support, develop, celebrate, and uplift underrepresented leaders. The SLE is a pioneering leadership development approach that stands out in its commitment to inclusivity and empowerment in leadership. While we have designed the SLE to dismantle leadership stereotypes and transform conventional leadership paradigms, the approach is all about empowering YOU.

The SLE invites you to explore your internal motivations more deeply, identify your unique Leadership Type, and activate your external power. The SLE is more than just a tool to help you better understand yourself and others to lead more authentically and effectively. It sets you on the path toward taking action to build a strong, authentic Leadership Brand, one that enables you to achieve your greatest impact both personally and professionally.

Through our analysis of the hundreds of individual Leadership Brands we have built through our work at BREAKTHRU, we have identified the 12 most salient Leadership Types and strategically placed them within the SLE to inspire additional leadership insights and opportunities. Each Leadership Type represents a unique set of leadership characteristics, qualities, and behaviors based on that leader's internal motivation and greatest external power. Each of the 12 Leadership Types is inspired by the theory of brand archetypes (more on that in the final chapter), yet we have updated them to be more inclusive, empowering, and actionable.

Furthermore, we believe that just as product, service, and company **brands** that embody familiar archetypes tend to better connect and resonate more deeply with their target audiences, individuals who lean into their Leadership Type can better relate to and communicate with others. From there, they can build their Leadership Brand by turning their inner motivation into external impact within their teams, organizations, industries, communities, and world.

Brands

Quick Definition:

A brand is more than its visual identity; it is a comprehensive representation of a company's values, mission, and connection with its audience. It transcends the functional attributes of products or services to establish a deep, emotional, and psychological connection with consumers, influencing their choices and loyalty.

Three Key Things to Know About This Topic:

- Brands have evolved from simple markers of quality to complex symbols that embody shared values and cultural identities, influencing both consumer behavior and societal trends.
- The "three Vs" of brand identity—values, verbal identity, and visual identity—work together to create a compelling narrative that resonates with consumers on multiple levels, fostering loyalty and differentiating the brand in a crowded marketplace.
- In today's digital age, a brand's interaction with consumers through online platforms is crucial. Effective digital engagement requires a consistent and strategic approach to reinforce brand identity and build strong relationships with consumers or users.

Why You Should Care About This Topic As a Leader:

Understanding and leveraging the power of brands is crucial for any leader seeking to effectively navigate a competitive market. A strong product, company, or service brand can command a premium, attract and retain loyal customers, influence broader cultural and social trends, and enhance the organization's impact on the community and the industry.

To learn more about this topic,
visit leadershiptypes.com/resources/brands/
or scan QR code:

Beyond just superficial categorization, the SLE delves deep into the psychology of leadership, offering insights into what motivates leaders to think, feel, and act in the ways that they do. Most importantly, it explores how each Leadership Type best relates to, communicates with, and motivates others. The SLE pushes leaders to think bigger when it comes to their greatest external powers and goals for impact—their full spectrum of possibilities—rather than fit themselves into a box. Your Leadership Type can evolve based on how your motivation evolves as a human, so the model is also a dynamic tool you can revisit based on your career or life stage and as your goals change.

As leaders navigate the complexities of organizational dynamics, interpersonal relationships, and self-growth, it becomes essential for them to have a firm grasp on their own Leadership Type and an understanding of the Leadership Types of those they lead, work for, and engage with. Leadership Types equip leaders to face challenges with confidence, **authenticity**, and a clear vision.

Authenticity

Quick Definition:

Authenticity in leadership refers to leaders being true to their values and beliefs while fostering an open, honest, and ethical environment within their organizations. This approach enhances trust, encourages open communication, and aligns personal and organizational values, contributing to more effective and humane management.

Three Key Things to Know About This Topic:
- Authentic leaders promote a workplace culture that values transparency and integrity, which enhances employee engagement and fosters a sense of trust and security.
- By being true to their values and encouraging diverse viewpoints, authentic leaders improve decision-making processes, ensuring that decisions are not only effective but also ethically sound.
- Authentic leadership is crucial for navigating change and uncertainty, as it ensures that leaders act with integrity and consistency, fostering organizational resilience and adaptability.

Why You Should Care About This Topic As a Leader:

Embracing authenticity in your leadership style is essential because it builds a foundation of trust and respect that is crucial for effective leadership. It not only promotes a positive and inclusive workplace culture but also enhances your ability to lead through challenges by remaining true to core values and principles. Authentic leadership also attracts and retains top talent, as employees are more likely to commit to leaders and organizations that demonstrate genuine care and integrity.

To learn more about this topic,
visit leadershiptypes.com/resources/authenticity/
or scan QR code:

Here are more ways of thinking about how Leadership Types can help you lead more effectively:

- ✔ A blueprint guiding your actions, decisions, and interactions to create a coherent leadership identity
- ✔ A compass pointing you toward your "true north" and your greatest potential impact on your leadership journey
- ✔ A personalized lens enabling you to view your own and others' strengths, values, and even vulnerabilities with unparalleled clarity
- ✔ A filter helping you communicate your thinking, plans, and ideas more lucidly
- ✔ A mirror reflecting the leader you are and casting visions for yourself and others
- ✔ A beacon guiding your decision-making
- ✔ A GPS for building and honing your brand as a leader

While traditional leadership models often offer generic advice and strategies, Leadership Types speak to the individual. They consider the nuanced shades of a leader's personality, ensuring that guidance is tailored and relevant. It is not just about leading but about leading authentically. By identifying their Leadership Types, individuals and organizations can craft strategies and make decisions that align with their core values and strengths while avoiding the pitfalls of inauthenticity.

Patriarchal systems, which historically have been rooted in power dynamics and biases, often stifle diverse voices and leadership styles. Leadership Types serve to challenge **societal systems** by paving the way for a more inclusive leadership environment where each style is celebrated, not sidelined. Moreover, shedding light on different leadership strengths and values challenges age-old leadership stereotypes, making room for voices that were previously overshadowed. They help guide forward-thinking organizations to reshape their leadership dynamics, foster a greater sense of belonging, and encourage resiliency in their underrepresented leaders. In turn, they reap the benefits of varied perspectives and approaches.

Societal Systems

Quick Definition:

Societal systems such as patriarchy, meritocracy, and systemic racism significantly influence leadership by shaping who holds leadership positions and how leadership roles are perceived and enacted. These systems affect the distribution of power and leadership effectiveness, making an understanding of their historical and current impacts essential for fostering equitable and effective leadership today.

Three Key Things to Know About This Topic:
- The historical development of societal systems like patriarchy and systemic racism has created enduring barriers that impact leadership diversity and dynamics, influencing who rises to leadership and the styles that are valued.
- These societal systems continue to shape leadership opportunities and effectiveness, often reinforcing traditional power structures and limiting diversity within leadership ranks.
- Understanding the pervasive effects of these systems is crucial for dismantling barriers and promoting a more inclusive approach to leadership that values diverse perspectives and equitable opportunities.

Why You Should Care About This Topic As a Leader:

As a leader or future leader, recognizing and actively addressing the influence of societal systems on leadership is vital. By doing so, you can help dismantle outdated and unfair practices, contribute to a more equitable distribution of leadership roles, and foster a leadership culture that is inclusive, diverse, and effective. This commitment not only promotes justice and equality but also enhances organizational performance by incorporating a wide range of experiences and viewpoints.

To learn more about this topic,
leadershiptypes.com/resources/societal-systems
or scan QR code:

By recognizing and valuing a multitude of leadership styles, Leadership Types democratize leadership, emphasizing that qualities such as empathy, collaboration, and nurturing—qualities often dismissed or undervalued in traditional leadership development—are just as vital and impactful as decisiveness, dominance, and assertiveness. In the SLE, leaders who possess traits that break stereotypes are seen not as anomalies but as invaluable assets who bring their unique strengths to the table and embolden those who might feel their leadership style does not fit the conventional mold.

The beauty of Leadership Types lies in their universal applicability. Whether you are spearheading a grassroots movement or are at the helm of a multinational corporation, your Leadership Type remains a steady and durable way to center yourself. Understanding it helps you recognize that while the contexts and challenges of leadership might vary, the essence of a leader—their character, values, and motivations—remains constant.

By giving leaders this deep-rooted understanding of themselves, Leadership Types equip them to face any leadership challenge with confidence, authenticity, and a clear vision. Let's look at how the Leadership Types come together and relate to one another to form the SLE.

The SLE is visually depicted as a wheel of diverse Types, with layers of elements that provide insights from the innermost aspects of the leader to their outermost opportunities. We start at the very center of the model, which symbolizes the inner "core" of the leader. Radiating out from this core are their internal motivations: what inspires them to think, decide, act, and behave in the ways that they do. Motivation is a critical but often overlooked aspect of leadership and leadership development. Leadership relies upon the leader's motivation to make decisions and take actions and their ability to motivate others to do the same. If we can understand what truly motivates us and others (beyond Maslow's hierarchy of needs and beyond fear and greed), we can begin to understand and unlock the power of authentic leadership.

Motivation is the invisible hand that pushes us to act, strive, and achieve. Our motivations are like an inner compass guiding our decisions and interactions, both subtle and significant. It is not just a one-off feeling that gets us out of bed in the morning or compels us to take on a new project. Rather, motivation is a complex interplay of intrinsic and extrinsic factors that influence our ongoing behaviors and ultimately define who we are and what we do. Motivation can evolve over time and change in response to context, including current opportunities and challenges. Understanding motivation is critical, then, because it fuels the actions that affect our performance, engagement, and satisfaction in various aspects of life and leadership.

When developing the Leadership Types framework, we carefully considered the multifaceted nature of motivation to create a model that is as comprehensive as it is digestible, one that is more dynamic and adaptive relative to other models that tend to be more static. So, though these motivations might seem simple by nature, you will soon see how multifaceted they are and how they show up in various ways. Each one extends out from the center of the SLE to a unique Leadership Type. We intentionally named the Leadership Types in a way that would feel inclusive, expansive, relevant, and actionable to today's leaders and changemakers.

As you move from the Leadership Types to the outer ring of the SLE, you are symbolically moving from the space of the leader's internal motivation toward the limitless space of the leader's external impact. You are moving from a place of inward self-focus to a place of outward perspective of others. In essence, you are moving from the intangible to the more tangible and into a space where you can tap into your greatest power, realize your potential, and make a meaningful impact.

The SLE is organized into four primary quadrants of external powers that leaders can display: to create, to awaken, to unite, and to structure. The selection of these four categories was not arbitrary. Each power quadrant encapsulates broad areas of human aspiration and action that have been widely studied and validated in motivational psychology, including Carl Jung's four "cardinal orientations" of human behavior:[9]

1. Ego → to make one's presence known and admired
2. Order → to maintain structure in societal settings
3. Social → to foster genuine connections with others
4. Freedom → to break free from physical and psychological limits

Each quadrant is intended to reflect different aspects of the aspirations, ambitions, and greatest impacts leaders can have, from the innate desire to bring about change to the compelling need for community and human connection, the maintenance of structure and control of the environment, and the ethereal but potent drive to envision and inspire a better future.

Before we explore each of the 12 Leadership Types in greater detail, there are two additional aspects of how the SLE model was intentionally designed that are important to mention.

First, each Leadership Type is influenced by its two adjacent Leadership Types. These "internal influences" are akin to the subtle hues that add depth to a primary color; they are the adjacent leadership characteristics and qualities that give richness and versatility to your leadership approach. This component of the SLE model recognizes that while you may have a predominant Leadership Type, you are not confined to it. Your Leadership Type is not one-dimensional. Rather, it is the combination of your Leadership Type's central characteristics and the subtle yet influential traits of the adjacent Types that creates a multifaceted and adaptive leadership style. We consider these influences to be internal because they stem from your inherent qualities and preferences and subtly shape your decisions and behaviors in various contexts. By recognizing and harnessing these influences,

---

9. Lily Yuan, "Guide: 12 Jungian Archetypes as Popularized by the Hero and the Outlaw," Personality Psychology, January 3, 2022, https://personality-psychology.com/guide-12-jungian-archetypes/.

you can navigate complex leadership situations with greater agility, cater to diverse needs, and cultivate an approach that is both nuanced and impactful.

Second, each Leadership Type is also influenced by the Leadership Type diametrically opposing it on the model. This "external amplifier" provides a crucial counterbalance that can propel you out of your comfort zone and into realms of unexpected growth. While the internal influences blend seamlessly with a leader's primary traits, the external amplifier can challenge and stretch that leader's natural tendencies. This might manifest as a tension between innate inclinations and the need to adopt strategies that are not instinctive but necessary for comprehensive leadership and evolution. Acknowledging and embracing your external amplifier equips you with a broader range of tools to address challenges, drive change, and influence effectively across a broader spectrum of scenarios. This dynamic tension can become a source of energy that spurs innovation, fosters resilience, and ultimately enhances your ability to positively impact their environment.

Which Leadership Type are you? The answer is reflected not just in your decisions, strategies, and public image but also in your deeper yet often unexplored motivations, aspirations, and future potential.

As we embark on this journey together, the SLE will serve as a map that is here to guide you and inspire you to explore. As I walk you through the four power quadrants, I will spotlight the trio of Leadership Types each power quadrant encompasses. I will introduce you to their unique attributes, distinct motivations, and the impact they typically wield, whether in a boardroom, a social setting, or a transformative movement. This nuanced exploration aims to describe and help you resonate with one or more Leadership Types and offers actionable insights for your personal leadership journey.

Leadership Types and the SLE are also powerful tools for reflection and growth. As you become exposed to and familiar with them, you will discover your values and motivations as well as those of others, allowing you to find inspiration and lead with more confidence and support.

Beyond individual leadership development, organizations can foster environments where diversity thrives by encouraging leaders to delve into their Leadership Types and embrace their associated values and traits. When leaders recognize and value the unique strengths of different Leadership Types, it sends a powerful message throughout the organization that every leadership style, irrespective of how it deviates from traditional norms, has inherent worth and contributes to collective success. Such a mindset naturally leads to a more inclusive, and ultimately more effective, form of leadership.

The ripple effects of this shift go beyond leadership roles, creating a culture that values individuality, promotes equity, and consistently challenges and redefines outdated notions of what effective leadership looks like. Organizations that embrace the SLE and promote its application will spearhead the transformation of the leadership landscape.

MEET THE 12 LEADERSHIP TYPES

Equipped with a better sense of how and why the SLE was designed, we are now ready to delve into each of the 12 Leadership Types spanning the four power quadrants: to create, to awaken, to unite, and to structure.

Each Leadership Type begins with a story about one of the standout leaders we have had the opportunity to collaborate with through our leadership and personal brand development work at BREAKTHRU. Each story is meant to give you a sense of how an individual's purpose, mission, vision, values, and internal motivation can be uniquely expressed through their leadership and the impact that this leadership makes on others. You will see a range of barrier-breaking leaders featured, from the business to the sports and the nonprofit realms. You most likely have not heard of most of these leaders, but the proof of their impact is undisputable. We hope these great leaders serve as an inspiration to you and remind you of the potential for impact that exists in us all.

Each Leadership Type is then broken down into dimensions that focus on the following key elements:

- → Internal Motivation
- → Greatest External Power
- → How They Best Communicate and Relate
- → Key Leadership Behaviors
- → Why The World Needs Them
- → Calls to Action
- → Examples of Leaders Who Embody Them

Let's get started.

QUADRANT 1:
THE POWER TO CREATE

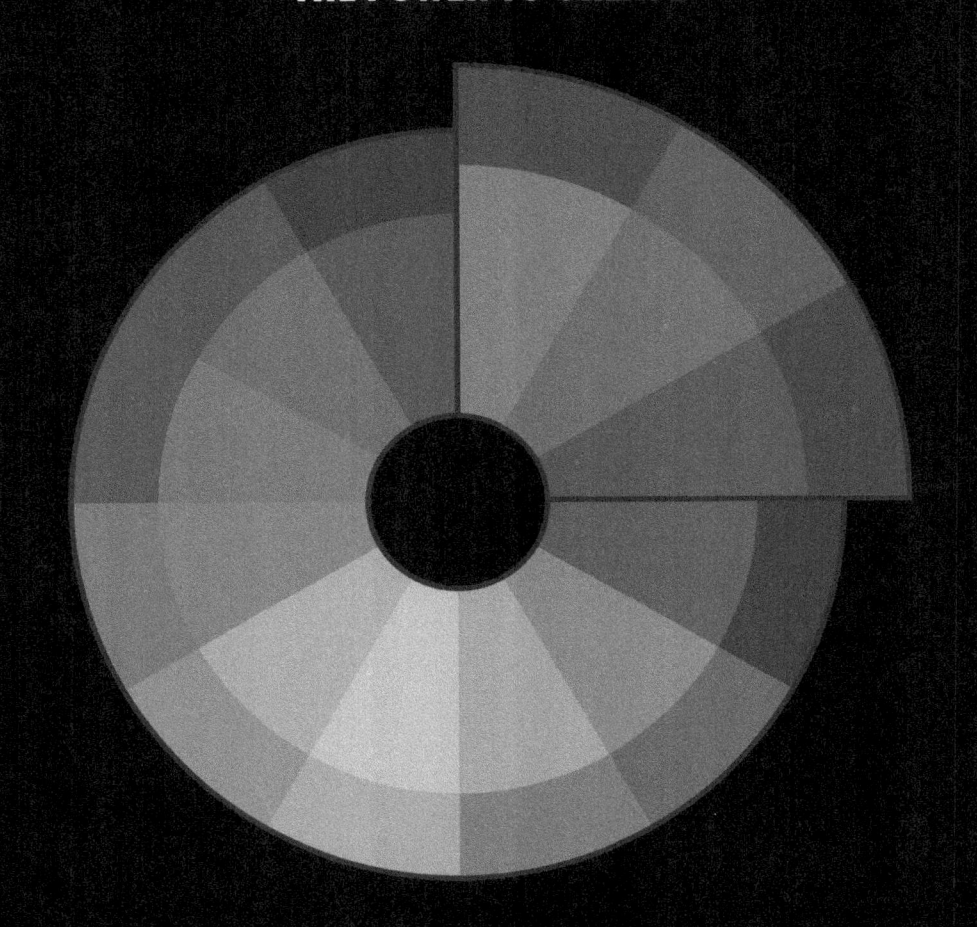

In an era characterized by rapid change and constant evolution, there exists a group of leaders who keep a steady eye on the future, seeing not just what is, but what could be. These leaders are the architects of novel ideas, the drivers of transformative change, and the pioneers who usher in new eras of thought and design. Their mission is less about maintaining the status quo and more about breaking molds, designing futures, and painting canvases of tomorrow's world.

Within this realm of creativity lies the power to create—a motivational force driving The Visionary, The Legend, and The Innovator. These leaders are driven by an insatiable desire to build, innovate, and bring to life visions that were previously only in their imaginations. They seek to mold the abstract into the tangible, turning dreams into realities and redefining what is possible.

The Visionary has the power to create by architecting future systems. They dream in vivid colors and are always a step ahead, painting grand pictures of the future and inspiring others to see their unique perspectives.

The Legend has the power to create by revitalizing and enhancing structures. They embody the spirit of unwavering commitment, translating visions into action. They do not just dream; they rally resources, people, and energies to make those dreams tangible.

The Innovator has the power to create by showcasing creative potential. They are the alchemists of this group, merging knowledge with creativity. They delve deep into their domain, seeking ways to revolutionize it, and they constantly push boundaries to make their innovative visions come to life.

Together, these leaders epitomize the essence of creation, proving that with imagination, determination, and expertise, the horizons of what we can achieve are boundless.

Visionary

Visionaries are the forerunners of the future, adeptly bridging aspirations with reality. As dream weavers, they paint vivid and compelling pictures of what could be, drawing others into a world rich with potential.

Motivation
Realization through connecting dots

Motto
"Actualize dreams"

Promise
To architect the future

Fear
Myopia

Tone of Voice
- Futuristic
- Compelling
- Expansive
- Inspirational
- Moving

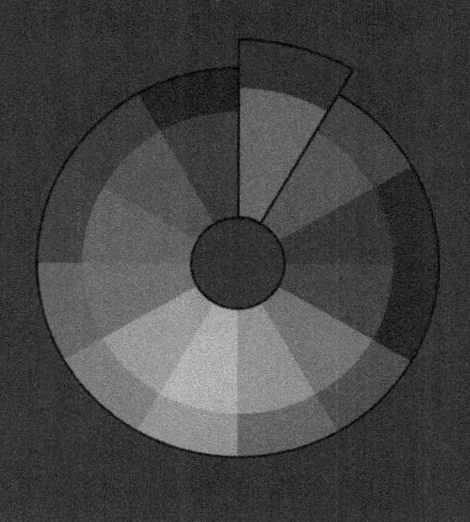

Power
To create
- Architecting future systems
- Cultivating inspiration in others
- Provoking forward-thinking ideas
- Rallying around a shared vision

Influences
Redemption and Knowledge
These motivations of The Legend and The Guide influence The Visionary's thoughts and actions.

Amplifier
Relationships
Combined with this internal motivation of The Connector, Visionaries can expand their thinking and find opportunities for growth.

MEET THE VISIONARY

As I dream big, I try to be accountable to myself, to my team, and to my family in terms of taking action and really beginning to build the building blocks of whatever that vision might be.

~Charles Inokon, cofounder and CEO of Cadence Cash

With over twenty-five years of experience as a founder, global legal advisor, strategic business executive, and chief operating officer for companies running the world's most critical systems of supply and demand, **Charles Inokon** has seen the inequities within those systems firsthand and is on a mission to change them.

As a trusted general counsel and independent business consultant, Inokon guides top-level executives, advises board members, and steers leadership teams in systematic transformations. His entrepreneurial spirit drives him to not only explore these systems but also actively reshape their disparities. This pursuit of equitable change has led to his latest venture.

As the cofounder and CEO of Cadence Cash, Inokon has embarked on a groundbreaking initiative. Recognizing the vast disparities in the financial world, Cadence Cash is dedicated to providing funding to small businesses, with an emphasis on supporting women and minority-owned enterprises. But Cadence Cash is not just a lender. It stands as a steadfast ally to these businesses, nurturing their aspirations with working capital, expert coaching, and vital networking opportunities. Cadence Cash encapsulates Inokon's unyielding commitment to leveling the playing field in the world of business finance.

Inokon continuously builds technological innovations that change the face of ownership and consumerism for global systems in crisis. Influenced by his learnings as an executive who leads critical systems, such as food supply at US Foods and homeland security at OSI Systems, he focuses on industries our livelihood depends on most: the supply chain, logistics, and finance. Inokon's data-driven solutions focus on ensuring equitable access and quality of food and capital while diversifying those leading the way in supplying these essential goods and services. While underrepresented and unconsidered groups benefit from inclusion, the global economy benefits from accelerated demand, increased business for suppliers, and the addition of new jobs to keep up with growth.

With the emotional intelligence of a relational leader and the negotiating power of a practicing attorney, Inokon is uniquely positioned to lead meaningful change. Inspired by his successful immigrant parents, his resilient and entrepreneurial wife, and his growing daughters, Inokon is a passionate, socially minded innovator out to make society's most critical systems work for everyone.

Inspired by Inokon's story, let's dive deeper into his Leadership Type: The Visionary.

Brief Description of The Visionary

Visionaries are the forerunners of the future, adeptly bridging aspirations with reality. As dream weavers, they paint vivid and compelling pictures of what could be, drawing others into a world rich with potential.

Internal Motivation of The Visionary

The Visionary's strongest internal motivation is realization, or turning dreams into reality. The Visionary's words, decisions, and actions can also be influenced by knowledge and redemption, the internal motivations of their adjacent Leadership Types (The Guide and The Legend).

The greatest fear of The Visionary is myopia, which in a leadership context refers to a shortsightedness or a narrow focus that prevents the leader from seeing the bigger picture or long-term consequences of their decisions or actions. Myopia can hinder The Visionary's innovation, stifle their growth, and lead to missed opportunities.

An energizing force or amplifier for The Visionary is relationships, the internal motivation of their opposite Type on the SLE, The Connector. For The Visionary, this opposing motivation can expand their thinking and be an opportunity for growth because they know that dreams can find wings in The Connector's drive for collaboration. The Connector's spirit inspires The Visionary to spread their ideas, ensuring their visions touch every horizon.

Greatest External Power of The Visionary

The Visionary's greatest external power is to create by architecting a better future. They can achieve this by cultivating inspiration in others, provoking forward-thinking ideas, and rallying around a shared vision.

How The Visionary Best Communicates & Relates

The Visionary uniquely recognizes potential for growth in others. They instill confidence in others that solutions are within reach, they align the individual goals of others with the overarching vision, and they promote forward-thinking in others.

To best communicate with others, here is what The Visionary does:

- ✔ Articulates a compelling future, boosting the aspirations of others
- ✔ Shares inspirational ideas, making concepts engaging and motivating
- ✔ Rallies people around a powerful and clear vision, demonstrating what can be achieved
- ✔ Provokes thought with forward-thinking perspectives

To best relate to others, here is what The Visionary does:

- ✔ Bonds over shared future goals

- ✔ Engages resources that facilitate the realization of aspirations
- ✔ Communicates passion to energize and inspire
- ✔ Forms strategic partnerships to strengthen and support their forward-thinking goals

Key Leadership Behaviors of The Visionary

The Visionary possesses a clear vision and is growth-centric. They consistently demonstrate a commitment to turning vision into reality, they embody the values and future aspirations of their team or organization, and they are open to new ideas and approaches.

In response to problems and obstacles, The Visionary embraces systems thinking, a holistic approach to analysis whereby they view problems as part of a wider, dynamic system and seek to understand how things influence one another as part of this greater system. They leverage creativity and an open mind to devise comprehensive solutions. They efficiently leverage resources to overcome obstacles to these solutions by focusing on the bigger picture, maintaining a long-term perspective, leveraging challenges as opportunities for growth, and promoting an optimistic outlook.

To inform their decision-making, The Visionary weighs the options against the long-term vision and potential impact. They consider innovative solutions over traditional methods, and they value foresight from and planning by others.

In tandem with this growth-centric mindset, The Visionary shapes spaces by promoting curiosity, encouraging continuous improvement, and genuinely valuing every idea. They seek to align values with trendsetting goals and bring others along on the journey. When they encounter bias and barriers, The Visionary overcomes them by encouraging diversity of thought to enrich a shared vision, breaking down silos and encouraging cross-functional collaboration, and leading change initiatives to overcome institutional barriers.

These combined traits allow The Visionary to thrive in leadership roles that require big-picture thinking and strategic planning, where innovation and foresight are essential. They excel in positions that can influence and steer future trends and directions.

Why the World Needs More Visionaries

- To inspire progress
- To anticipate opportunities and obstacles
- To turn abstract ideas into concrete realities
- To propel people and ideas into the future

Calls to Action If You Are a Visionary

Embracing The Visionary Leadership Type often means embarking on transformative journeys that promise significant change. While your capacity to dream big is unparalleled, ensuring these dreams are anchored in actionable strategies is essential. By marrying your expansive visions with concrete steps, you have the potential to drive organizational and societal reinvention, crafting a legacy that stands the test of time. Here are some specific calls to action and ways you can realize your full leadership potential as a Visionary:

→ Foster a Culture of Innovation
  As a Visionary leader, your strength lies in reimagining and reshaping the future. To bring your transformative ideas to life, cultivate an environment where innovation is not just encouraged but celebrated. Here are the steps to take:
  - Encourage a continuous flow of ideas by setting up regular brainstorming and ideation sessions.
  - Recognize and reward creative solutions and innovative approaches within your team.
  - Dedicate resources to research and development, ensuring that groundbreaking ideas are nurtured and have room to evolve.

→ Lead by Your Vision

Your unique gift is the ability to see a brighter, better tomorrow. It is imperative to ensure that this vision is not just a dream but serves as a clear roadmap for your organization. Here are the steps to take:
- Clearly articulate your vision to the team, making sure it is communicated effectively across all levels.
- Align organizational goals and key performance indicators with the larger vision, ensuring cohesive movement toward the desired future.
- Periodically reassess and refine the vision based on feedback and evolving circumstances, ensuring it remains relevant and actionable.

→ Build Resilience Against Fear

While your Visionary outlook is a powerful asset, it might occasionally be tempered by concerns of unintended consequences or stagnation. Addressing these fears head-on will empower you to lead with confidence. Here are the steps to take:
- Engage in risk-assessment exercises, preparing for potential challenges and outlining proactive solutions.
- Foster an organizational mindset that views setbacks as learning opportunities, ensuring that challenges are met with resilience and growth.
- Prioritize continuous learning, ensuring you stay updated with the latest trends and shifts and minimize the chances of stagnation.

Visionaries You Should Know

Mae Jemison's career as an astronaut, physician, and science educator embodies the essence of a Visionary. As the first African American woman to travel in space, Jemison broke new ground in space exploration. Her subsequent work in science education and advocacy for science literacy demonstrates her commitment to inspiring future generations and expanding the boundaries of human knowledge and potential.

A defining moment in Jemison's career as a Visionary occurred in 1992 when she flew into space aboard the space shuttle *Endeavour*. This mission marked a historic moment, not only as a personal achievement for Jemison but also as a significant milestone in the history of space exploration, symbolizing the breaking of racial and gender barriers. Following her space mission, Jemison founded The Jemison Group and the Dorothy Jemison Foundation for Excellence, focusing on science literacy and promoting technology in everyday life. Through these endeavors, Jemison has continued to inspire and educate, playing a crucial role in shaping the future of science and space exploration.

Another great example of The Visionary Leadership Type is **Reshma Saujani**. As the founder of Girls Who Code, Saujani has demonstrated an extraordinary ability to see a better future and work tirelessly toward it. Her initiative bridges the gender gap in technology by equipping young women with the necessary skills and confidence to thrive in tech careers. Saujani's approach involves designing systems (such as educational programs), mobilizing resources (through partnerships and community engagement), and manifesting her ideas into impactful solutions.

A notable story of Saujani's Visionary leadership is the inception and growth of Girls Who Code. Recognizing the stark gender disparity in technology fields, she launched the organization to address this gap head-on. Girls Who Code began as a small initiative but quickly grew into a major movement that is now impacting thousands of young women across the United States and beyond. This initiative provided coding education and fostered a sense of community and empowerment among its participants. Saujani's vision transformed a challenge into an opportunity, creating a platform for young women to develop their skills and confidence, thereby reshaping the tech industry's future. Her work is a testament to her Visionary leadership, embodying the motto "There's a solution for everything" and demonstrating a deep commitment to turning her Visionary ideas into reality.

Other examples of leaders who embody The Visionary Leadership Type include **Grace Hopper,** for her groundbreaking work in computer science and her vision of modern computing; **Maya Angelou,** for her ability to transform personal experiences into universal truths and inspire others through her writing and activism; **Marie Curie**, for her pioneering work in radioactivity and her achievements in science that transformed our understanding of the world; **Octavia Butler,** for her thought-provoking science fiction works that challenged and expanded the boundaries of the genre; **Katherine Johnson**, the pioneering NASA mathematician and a barrier-breaker for women and people of color; and **Kumi Naidoo,** for his relentless pursuit of social justice and environmental conservation, demonstrating a Visionary approach to global activism that bridges the gap between human rights and the urgent need to address climate change.

LEGEND

Legends are reformers. They have an intrinsic desire to articulate opportunities for meaningful change and improvement in existing structures. They are steadfast in their goals and feel a shared responsibility to drive betterment, improvement, and positive transformation.

Motivation
Redemption through changing the trajectory

Motto
"Enhance the now"

Promise
To lead meaningful efforts with courage

Fear
Insignificance

Tone of Voice
- Resolute
- Proactive
- Resilient
- Courageous
- Independent

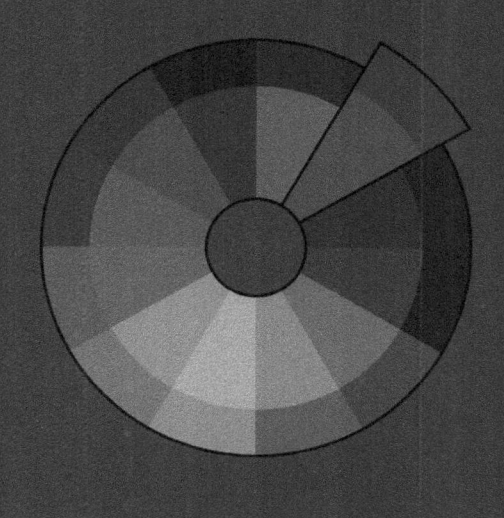

Power
To create
- Revitalizing and enhancing structures
- Exemplifying courageous action
- Driving reform
- Maintaining proactive advancement

Influences
Realization and Expression
These motivations of The Visionary and The Innovator influence The Legend's thoughts and actions.

Amplifier
Altruism
Combined with this internal motivation of The Protector, Legends can expand their thinking and find opportunities for growth.

MEET THE LEGEND

*I believe in and am trying to build a legacy out of love.
It's all about putting love first and ensuring that everything I do honors that principle.*

~Wanda Cooper Jones, founder of the
Ahmaud Arbery Foundation

A mother, founder, advocate, and business professional, **Wanda Cooper Jones** is turning a moment of hate into a movement of love. After the tragic, racially charged murder of her son Ahmaud Arbery, Cooper Jones's resilience and mission to keep her son's name alive led to the start of the Ahmaud Arbery Foundation.

In addition to impacting the community with her son's legacy, Cooper Jones has committed to making significant change and accelerating progress. Her activism has led to the passing of Georgia's hate crime legislation in 2020 and the repeal of Georgia's citizen's arrest law in 2021.

Adding to her influence on state and federal platforms, Cooper Jones continues to support and impact her local community through the Ahmaud Arbery Foundation's scholarship program. With Cooper Jones's personal belief that education is the key to sustainable advancement and positive opportunities for youth and communities, the scholarship awards high school seniors of Ahmaud's alma mater and assists with their higher education aspirations.

Cooper Jones is also providing strength and support to mothers who have lost children and experienced tragedy. She embodies the saying, "Where there is a will, there is a way," and she is a testament that there is life and joy after major devastation. Cooper Jones is not just a mom but a supportive, victorious leader who is fighting to both deliver and be the good news. She aims to spark change through Ahmaud's legacy and to promote love, empathy, and equality for all—even when it is hard.

Inspired by Cooper Jones's story, let's dive deeper into her Leadership Type: The Legend.

Brief Description of The Legend

Legends are reformers. They have an intrinsic desire to articulate opportunities for meaningful change and improvement in existing structures. They are steadfast in their goals and feel a shared responsibility to drive betterment, improvement, and positive transformation.

Internal Motivation of The Legend

The Legend's strongest internal motivation is redemption, or changing the trajectory. Legends have an intrinsic desire to improve conditions and outcomes for the greater good. The Legend's words, decisions, and actions can also be influenced by realization and expression, the internal motivations of their adjacent Leadership Types (The Visionary and The Innovator).

The greatest fear of The Legend is insignificance, which in a leadership context refers to a lack of influence, impact, or relevance. Insignificance can threaten The Legend's desire to leave a lasting legacy.

An energizing force or amplifier for The Legend is altruism, the internal motivation of their opposite Type on the SLE, The Protector. For The Visionary, this opposing motivation can expand their thinking and be an opportunity for growth because The Protector's unifying spirit offers them fervent support. The Protector's loyalty ensures The Legend's causes resonate, blending passion with engagement.

Greatest External Power of The Legend

The Legend's greatest external power is to create by driving reform through revitalizing and enhancing social structures. They exemplify courage and proactively work to find better solutions to the problems faced by others, cultivating excellence along the way.

How The Legend Best Communicates & Relates

The Legend empowers change. They encourage others to challenge existing paradigms or assumptions, and they foster a sense of relentless improvement. Their growth mindset is contagious.

To best communicate with others, here is what The Legend does:

- ✔ Articulates pathways for improvement and restoration
- ✔ Encourages critical reevaluation of established practices, fostering a mindset of constructive development
- ✔ Conveys with unwavering courage and conviction, inclining others toward impactful progress
- ✔ Focuses on practical and effective methods that emphasize hands-on approaches to enhance current situations

To best relate to others, here is what The Legend does:

- ✔ Engages with those committed to concrete and meaningful improvements
- ✔ Demonstrates unwavering courage and initiative, fostering trust and encouraging action
- ✔ Steers others toward achieving tangible results and pragmatic advancements
- ✔ Nurtures a culture of bravery and action, emboldening others to take steps in pursuit of betterment

Key Leadership Behaviors of The Legend

The Legend embodies purposeful and reformative leadership. They lead with a strong sense of purpose and accountability, staying true to the mission of reform and betterment. They are transparent about their intentions and the necessity for change, and they encourage others to adopt a limitless mindset about the future. Through all of this, The Legend can empower change and help others challenge existing paradigms.

When it comes to solving problems and overcoming obstacles, The Legend approaches problems as opportunities to grow and improve, challenging conventional wisdom to find novel solutions and taking calculated risks to effect meaningful change. They embrace complexity as a pathway to uncovering better systems or ways of doing things, and they overcome obstacles in this pathway by mobilizing resources, remaining focused on purpose, and leveraging resilience and determination to push through challenges.

To inform their decision-making, especially about the future, The Legend reflects on both their purpose and their past successes to make decisions by evaluating options based on the potential for long-term transformation. In consideration of the greater good, they seek to be strategic and intentional, prioritizing options that bring about systemic change.

In tandem with this intentional mindset, The Legend shapes spaces by celebrating excellence through setting and maintaining high standards for themselves and others, instilling a sense of shared responsibility. They encourage others to think critically and question the way things are, emphasizing the importance of making a lasting impact. When they encounter bias and barriers, they overcome them by actively working to dismantle outdated systems and prejudices, often leading initiatives that promote equity and systemic fairness. They also seek to recognize personal biases and continuously strive to overcome them, and they effectively build coalitions to challenge and shift the status quo.

These combined traits allow The Legend to thrive in leadership roles where transformation is needed and within organizations or movements that value reform and progress. They excel at the helm of initiatives that require vision and courageous leadership.

Why the World Needs More Legends

- To address and correct systemic issues and injustices
- To lead the charge in creating a better future for others

- To inspire and empower others to strive for a higher standard
- To ensure that progress and betterment are continuous and attainable

Calls to Action If You Are a Legend

As a Legend Leadership Type, your dynamism and passion are your greatest assets. While you have an innate drive to catalyze change, it is essential to combine that enthusiasm with structured strategies and execution. By investing in yourself, connecting with allies, and leveraging the right platforms, you can lead the charge effectively and create a lasting and meaningful impact. Here are some specific calls to action and ways you can realize your full leadership potential as a Legend:

→ Harness Platforms for Advocacy

As a Legend leader, you thrive when you can voice your transformative ideas and make a real difference. Capitalize on platforms that amplify your message and inspire others to rally behind your cause. Here are the action steps to take:
- Seek out and engage in conferences, panel discussions, and influential forums that align with your mission.
- Build relationships with industry groups and stakeholders who share your passion for change.
- Take the initiative on projects and campaigns you believe in, ensuring you are equipped with the necessary resources to succeed.

→ Prioritize Personal Growth

Your commitment to challenging the status quo and driving innovation requires continually refining your skills. Invest in yourself, and by extension the causes and objectives in which you believe. Here are the action steps to take:
- Identify key skills to enhance advocacy efforts and pursue relevant training or courses.

- Connect with seasoned advocates or thought leaders in your domain, learning from their journeys. Conversely, mentor emerging Legends to pay it forward.
- Foster a culture of feedback in your team or organization, valuing constructive insights that push you toward excellence.

→ Cultivate a Community of Allies

Your impact as a Legend is exponential when you are supported by a network of like-minded individuals. Building a cohesive community can significantly amplify your collective efforts. Here are the action steps to take:
- Organize or participate in networking events, creating spaces where people with aligned passions can converge.
- Initiate or join special interest groups that resonate with your mission, ensuring streamlined collaborative and strategic efforts.
- Dedicate resources to these groups by facilitating events, webinars, or campaigns that further the shared cause.

Legends You Should Know

With her formidable presence both on and off the tennis court, **Billie Jean King** stands as a towering figure embodying the essence of a Legend. Her victory in the "Battle of the Sexes" match against Bobby Riggs in 1973 was not just a win in tennis but a monumental victory for women's equality and social change. King's relentless advocacy for gender equality and her pioneering role in the establishment of the Women's Tennis Association showcase her unwavering commitment to reforming the sports industry and society at large. Her efforts have paved the way for equal prize money for men and women in tennis, a battle she has fought with perseverance and strategic acumen. King's actions reflect the core attributes of a Legend—driving reform, exemplifying courageous action, and maintaining a proactive advancement toward a more equitable future.

Beyond her achievements in leveling the playing field in sports, Billie Jean King extended her influence to her off-court endeavors, which have had a lasting impact on the cultural and social landscape. Her founding of the Billie Jean King Foundation and her active role in advocating for LGBTQIA+ rights demonstrate her broad vision for equality and her capacity to inspire change across different spheres of society. This defining aspect of her leadership is a testament to her ability to envision a better, more inclusive world and take bold actions to bring that vision to fruition. Through her life's work, King has both secured her legacy as a champion in the world of sports and solidified her status as a Legend in advocating for justice and equality, embodying the essence of leading meaningful efforts with courage and integrity.

Another great example of The Legend Leadership Type is **Stephen Mills**. He embodies the quintessence of a Legend through his innovative approach to information technology and unwavering commitment to empowering Indigenous communities. As the founder of Aqiwo, a firm that has seen a meteoric rise since its inception in 2002, Mills has not only achieved remarkable success in securing key clients within the defense and intelligence sectors but has also leveraged his position to advocate for meaningful change within and beyond his industry. His dedication to mentoring young Native Americans and encouraging them to pursue their entrepreneurial and professional aspirations speaks to his deep-rooted belief in the power of redemption and transformation. Mills's leadership style, characterized by resilience, courage, and a proactive stance toward challenging existing paradigms, aligns with the archetype of Legend leaders, who are committed to driving reform and enhancing structures for the betterment of society.

A defining moment that cements Mills's status as a Legend leader came when he spearheaded an initiative to integrate traditional Indigenous knowledge with cutting-edge technology solutions in environmental management projects for public sector clients. This innovative approach showcased the viability and value of Indigenous practices in contemporary contexts as well as set a precedent for how technology and tradition can intersect to create sustainable solutions for complex challenges. Mills's ability to bring this vision to fruition amid skepticism and resistance demonstrates his exceptional capacity to drive meaningful change. By marrying his ancestral heritage with his expertise in technology, Mills advanced his firm's mission and significantly contributed to the broader dialogue on environmental sustainability and cultural preservation. This moment of transformative leadership firmly established Mills as a figure who not only talks about change but actively instigates it, embodying the very essence of what it means to be a Legend leader.

Other examples of leaders who embody The Legend Leadership Type include **Rosa Parks**, for her pivotal role in propelling the civil rights movement; **Dr. Martin Luther King Jr.**, for his role as a civil rights leader and his advocacy for racial equality and nonviolent protest; **Malala Yousafzai**, the youngest Nobel Prize laureate, for her courageous advocacy for girls' education under the most daunting circumstances; **Ruth Bader Ginsburg**, for her tireless fight for gender equality and women's rights and her service as a Supreme Court justice who left an indelible mark on American law; **Roberto Clemente Walker**, for his humanitarian work and breaking baseball's racial and cultural barriers by being both a Hall of Fame athlete and a philanthropist; and **Shani Dhanda**, a leading global inclusion and disability activist.

INNOVATOR

Innovators are makers. They thrive in uncertainty and passionately strive to bring ideas to life. They have an inherent need to communicate through imaginative means, such as art, technology, design, or other forms of creation.

Motivation
Expression through creating something out of nothing

Motto
"Create wonders"

Promise
To bring imagination to life

Fear
Obsolescence

Tone of Voice
- Ideative
- Expressive
- Authentic
- Imaginative
- Creative

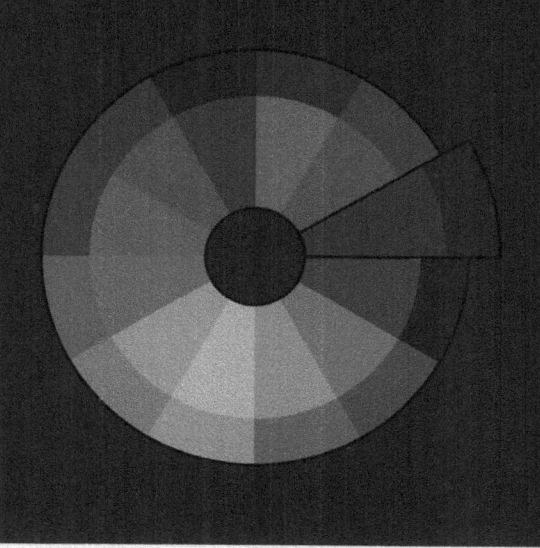

Power
To create
- Showcasing creative potential
- Bringing ideas to fruition
- Embracing novelty
- Fostering imaginative thinking

Influences
Redemption and Possibility
These motivations of The Legend and The Trailblazer influence The Innovator's thoughts and actions.

Amplifier
Understanding
Combined with this internal motivation of The Champion, Innovators can expand their thinking and find opportunities for growth.

MEET THE INNOVATOR

It is important that physicians innovate continuously, for the benefit of their patients, their practice, and their careers.

~Dr. Robin Vora, chair of ophthalmology,
The Permanente Medical Group

Dr. Robin Vora is a practicing cataract surgeon, a medical retina specialist, and an active advisor leading the healthcare industry into the future. Known to infuse every endeavor with unmatched energy and expertise, he is improving the level of care provided to patients by influencing a more transparent industry and guiding the next wave of industry Innovators to continue to raise the bar on patient-centric solutions.

For over a decade, Dr. Vora has shaped the future of eye care. As chair of ophthalmology for The Permanente Medical Group, he leads the mission of ensuring that 4.3 million Kaiser Permanente members benefit from the pinnacle of clinical and surgical eye care from a network of 250 ophthalmologists. He also acts as the chief of the department of ophthalmology in East Bay, where he directly oversees twenty ophthalmologists, twenty-five optometrists, and one hundred staff members on the Oakland and Richmond campuses. His depth of expertise as a medical retina specialist and cataract surgeon is evident in his comprehensive approach to treatment combined with a dedication to continuous learning and adaptation.

Dr. Vora's contributions to California extend beyond his clinical practice. His vision emphasizes a healthcare system underscored by transparency and innovation. This vision, coupled with his leadership, has shifted paradigms, influenced policy, and set benchmarks in ophthalmology. He is well-regarded not only for his direct contributions but also for his guidance to emerging healthcare entrepreneurs and influence on strategic boards. As an advisory board member, mentor, and public speaker, Dr. Vora is uplifting healthcare professionals, leading them to challenge the status quo to drive innovation, and building a legacy of transparent industry leadership.

Those familiar with Dr. Vora often describe him as deeply committed to his endeavors while adeptly maintaining a balanced lifestyle. His profound expertise and clear vision combined with his dedication to personal growth shine through in his medical contributions and beyond. He elevates the spheres he leads and paves the way for others to aspire and achieve.

Inspired by Dr. Vora's story, let's dive deeper into his Leadership Type: The Innovator.

Brief Description of The Innovator

Innovators are makers. They thrive in uncertainty and passionately strive to bring ideas to life. They have an inherent need to communicate through imaginative means, such as art, technology, design, or other forms of creation.

Internal Motivation of The Innovator

The Innovator's strongest internal motivation is expression, or creating something out of nothing. Innovators are "wired" to see possibilities beyond the present and are driven to transform the world by bringing inspired ideas to life. The Innovator's words, decisions, and actions can also be influenced by redemption and possibility, the internal motivations of their adjacent Leadership Types (The Legend and The Trailblazer).

The greatest fear of The Innovator is obsolescence, which in a leadership context refers to a leader becoming outdated or no longer relevant to, valued by, or sought after by others. Obsolescence can jeopardize The Innovator's competitive edge.

An energizing force or amplifier for The Innovator is understanding, the internal motivation of their opposite Type on the SLE, The Champion. For The Innovator, this opposing motivation can expand their thinking and be an opportunity for growth because they can find fresh ideas and direction in The Champion's call for justice. The Champion's sense of inclusion can ensure The Innovator that standards of fairness and integrity are upheld in their work.

Greatest External Power of The Innovator

The Innovator's greatest external power is to create by being open to and demonstrating possibilities, then actualizing the vision. They embrace novelty, encouraging divergent thinking in others to generate new ideas and then have the power to help bring them to life.

How The Innovator Best Communicates & Relates

The Innovator promotes experimentation. They encourage new ideas, turn others' ideas into tangible outcomes, and enrich processes with fresh takes and new approaches.

To best communicate with others, here is what The Innovator does:

- ✓ Encourages open-ended, imaginative ideation
- ✓ Leads dynamic brainstorming sessions, facilitating collaborative idea generation
- ✓ Translates novel ideas through art, technology, and design
- ✓ Uses visuals and prototypes to demonstrate concepts

To best relate to others, here is what The Innovator does:

- ✓ Bonds over shared creative passions, finding commonality in the joy of creation
- ✓ Integrates all perspectives across disciplines
- ✓ Encourages new ideas and approaches
- ✓ Values each individual's unique creative contributions

Key Leadership Behaviors of The Innovator

The Innovator embodies inventive and risk-tolerant approaches to leadership. They lead by example through experimentation and advocating for new ways of thinking or doing things, they encourage creative breakthroughs and champion fresh perspectives and creative approaches, and they work to ensure that organizational processes allow for creative freedom.

When it comes to solving problems and overcoming obstacles, The Innovator embraces design thinking, a creative and iterative approach to problem-solving that relies on observing with empathy how people interact with their environment. To find novel solutions, they explore multiple options and encourage collaboration and ideation. They possess the unique ability to break down complex problems into opportunities for growth, and they are adept at leveraging technology and trends to inform their problem-solving.

To inform their decision-making, The Innovator weighs options based on their potential to inspire or support innovation, considering the future implications and the evolution of ideas and embracing unconventional solutions and nontraditional approaches. They overcome obstacles by viewing them as opportunities for innovation, and they can channel their stress into creative energy and keep an open mind to possible solutions. Amid chaos and uncertainty, they can successfully maintain a creative mindset.

In tandem with this mindset, The Innovator shapes spaces by democratizing opportunities for creativity. They encourage experimentation, promote flexibility, and celebrate new ideas. To help mitigate bias and remove barriers for others, The Innovator actively challenges preconceived notions and traditional industry norms, promoting a culture where unconventional ideas are given a platform and implementing systems that reflect new ways of thinking.

These combined traits allow The Innovator to excel in environments that value change and progress. They have the potential to drive organizations forward through innovative products and services, influencing industries and sectors that value and benefit from creative thinking.

Why the World Needs More Innovators

- To push the boundaries of what is possible
- To bring new ideas and technologies into existence
- To inspire change and progress in every endeavor
- To lead the charge against mundanity and complacency

Calls to Action If You Are an Innovator

As an Innovator Leadership Type, your journey is marked by uncharted terrains and audacious goals. While your vision is vast, ensuring it is also grounded in practicality is essential. By blending your innovative spirit with structured strategies, you can mold your revolutionary ideas into transformative realities. Here are some specific calls to action and ways you can realize your full leadership potential as an Innovator:

→ Embrace an Experimental Mindset
As an Innovator, to maximize your potential you must cultivate an environment where experimentation is the norm, not the exception. Recognize that every failure is a stepping stone to your next groundbreaking idea. Here are the action steps to take:
- Launch your own "innovation labs" or set aside time for personal "hackathons" when you immerse yourself in exploring new concepts.
- Dedicate resources and seek mentorship to evolve your abstract thoughts into tangible solutions.
- Cultivate a personal philosophy that reframes failures as growth opportunities, with each setback guiding you toward a revolutionary breakthrough.

→ Encourage Diverse Input
While you do have a vision, your innovative ideas can benefit immensely from varied perspectives. Engage in collaborative brainstorming to refine and elevate your transformative visions. Here are the action steps to take:

- Organize regular brainstorming sessions, even if informally, inviting insights from different people and with a variety of expertise.
- Apply structured ideation techniques, such as design thinking, to harness the collective intelligence of these collaborations.
- Actively seek, value, and incorporate feedback to ensure your innovative pursuits are both pioneering and feasible.

→ Stay Ahead with Continuous Learning

As an Innovator, your edge lies in anticipating the future. To do so, it is vital to consistently immerse yourself in emerging trends, technological shifts, and evolving societal paradigms. Here are the action steps to take:
- Invest in your growth through specialized courses, workshops, and seminars that cater to emerging domains.
- Participate actively in industry events and gatherings, networking with peers and gleaning insights into the next big thing.
- Engage in discussions and dialogues on cutting-edge topics, from tech innovations to potential industry disruptions, ensuring you stay ahead of the curve.

Innovators You Should Know

Bozoma Saint John embodies The Innovator Leadership Type. Throughout her career in high-profile marketing roles, she has demonstrated a remarkable ability to actualize visionary ideas and embrace novel approaches. Her work, particularly in transforming brand images and enhancing consumer engagement through innovative marketing strategies, showcases her inherent need to communicate through creative means. Saint John's leadership is marked by her imaginative, expressive, and driven nature.

A notable highlight of Saint John's career was her role in the memorable 2014 Super Bowl halftime show featuring Bruno Mars, which she helped orchestrate while at PepsiCo. Her approach to this event was about creating not just a musical performance but a cultural moment that brought together music, technology, and audience engagement in innovative ways. This event highlighted her ability to think creatively, leveraging her creative acumen to produce a spectacular and highly talked-about event. Turning a traditional music performance into an immersive, memorable experience was a tangible demonstration of her motto "Give form to imagination," and it set a new standard in the field. Her impact in this role and others has consistently proven her to be a leader who not only embraces but thrives on innovation and creative thinking.

Another great example of The Innovator Leadership Type is **Dr. Daniel Hale Williams**, a standout in the field of medicine, particularly for performing one of the first successful open-heart surgeries. His groundbreaking work in the late nineteenth and early twentieth centuries paved the way for modern cardiac surgery. Beyond his surgical achievements, Williams also founded Provident Hospital, the first nonsegregated hospital in the United States, demonstrating his commitment to innovation in both medical practice and social equality.

The defining moment in Dr. Williams's career as an Innovator came in 1893 when he performed the first successful open-heart surgery on a patient with a stab wound to the chest at a time when such surgical procedures were unheard of and considered exceedingly risky. The success of this surgery marked a monumental achievement in medical history and established Dr. Williams as a pioneer in the field of cardiothoracic surgery. His innovative approach and successful procedure execution laid the groundwork for future advancements in heart surgery.

Other examples of leaders who embody The Innovator Leadership Type include **Richard Spikes**, an exemplary inventor holding multiple patents for inventions ranging from automobile improvements to innovations in the printing press; **Marina**

Abramovic, known for her boundary-pushing performance art; **Miuccia Prada**, a fashion icon known for merging fashion with other cultural forums including art, cinema, and design; **Michael Jordan**, the greatest—and perhaps most creative—basketball player of all time (as a kid from the Chicago suburbs, I say this as an indisputable fact), as well as an innovative business leader; **Anne Wojcicki**, entrepreneur and healthcare disruptor; **Issa Rae**, for transforming the entertainment landscape with her unique creative vision, leveraging the power of digital platforms to amplify underrepresented voices; and **Leila Janah**, a social entrepreneur who pioneered the idea of "giving work" as a sustainable solution to ending global poverty and founded companies that connect talented people in low-income countries to the digital economy.

QUADRANT 2:
THE POWER TO AWAKEN

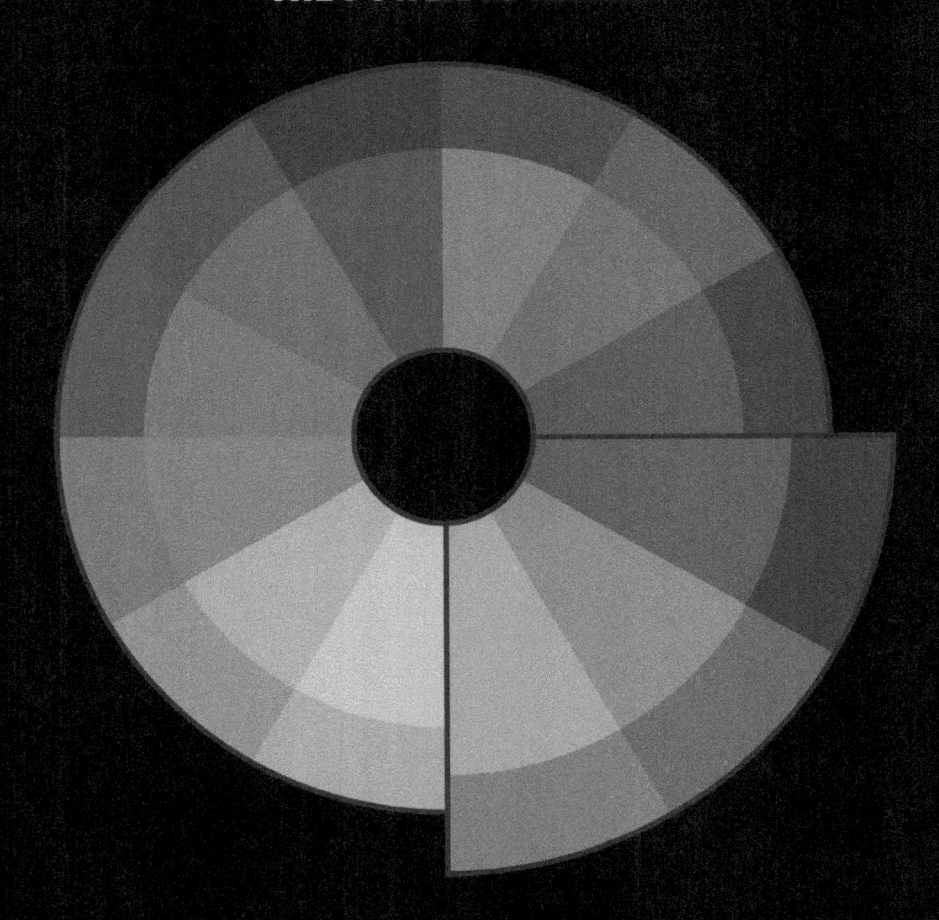

Leaders in the quadrant 2 domain are fueled by an inherent desire to awaken, enlighten, and invigorate the world around them. Their ambition is not just to exist but to transcend and elevate—to bring about moments of realization, bursts of enthusiasm, and a heightened sense of purpose both for themselves and those they influence.

Within this domain lies the power to awaken, embodied by the transformative Leadership Types of The Trailblazer, The Catalyst, and The Ignitor. Rather than treading worn paths, these leaders carve out new ones. They ignite change not only for the sake of disruption but for evolution, and they believe in the transformative power of positivity. They do not just lead; they awaken the potential, passion, and purpose in others.

The Trailblazer is not content with the status quo. They are always on the move, fueled by an insatiable curiosity and an indomitable spirit to challenge conventional wisdom and set new standards.

The Catalyst, on the other hand, is the agent of change. They understand that true transformation requires a mix of audacity and strategy. With a penchant for seeing the bigger picture, they maneuver through risks, turning potential pitfalls into stepping stones toward revolutionary change.

And then there is The Ignitor, the beacon of hope and happiness. Their presence is a reminder that amid the hustle and challenges, it is essential to celebrate life, embrace moments of joy, and spread that infectious energy to others.

Together, these leaders illuminate the path not merely by showing the way but by inspiring a deep-seated desire in others to discover, transform, and truly awaken.

Trailblazer

Trailblazers are seekers. They are driven by what could be rather than what currently is. They are the fearless adventurers at the frontier of the unknown, forming paths where others see dead ends and turning the impossible into the possible.

Motivation
Possibility of what could be

Motto
"Break boundaries"

Promise
To explore uncharted territories and ideas

Fear
Stagnation

Tone of Voice
- Fearless
- Agile
- Adventurous
- Experimental
- Pioneering

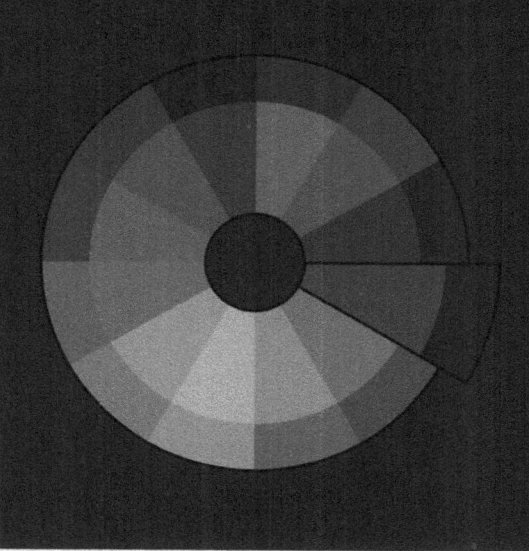

Power
To awaken
- Challenging conventions
- Encouraging experimentation
- Pioneering new paths
- Promoting possibilities

Influences
Expression and Liberation
These motivations of The Innovator and The Catalyst influence The Trailblazer's thoughts and actions.

Amplifier
Simplicity
Combined with this internal motivation of The Pathfinder, Trailblazers can expand their thinking and find opportunities for growth.

MEET THE TRAILBLAZER

People have said to me, "There's no way that will happen."
I've had the courage to go to spaces or places where people have said,
"You're going to fail," and I do it anyway.

~Dr. Amy Wilson, managing director of inclusion at the NCAA

A managing director, educator, and former student-athlete, Dr. Amy Wilson inspires others in both academia and sports to drive the action that contributes to a more equitable society. She does this by championing an intersectional lens, building cultures of belonging, and creating an anti-complacency movement.

Currently the managing director of inclusion at the National Collegiate Athletics Association (NCAA), Dr. Wilson is committed to and passionate about DEI and driving positive change through educating and empowering others. Through her actions and words, including authoring three national reports on Title IX and athletics, she bridges connections and challenges others to continue the fight for opportunities and equitable treatment of student-athletes and those who coach, teach, and lead them. She is proud of the equity and inclusive movement she leads and knows the work is never complete. Dr. Wilson fosters cultures of belonging, meeting people at the intersection of their identities to propel change and collaborative progress.

While in academia, Dr. Wilson encouraged revolution and ignited a call to action in others, both in the classroom and within the administration. At Illinois College she earned tenure as an associate professor of education, but she began her career at MacMurray College as an English instructor, influencing and impacting the athletic department and administration.

As Dr. Wilson is a former student-athlete, sports have been a part of her identity for most of her life, and she sees them as a way to stretch a person's potential. She appreciates that sports are accessible to many and that they allow opportunities to participate in inclusive teams while working toward a common goal.

She values sports as mental, physical, and spiritual experiences that have shaped her into the leader she is today.

Dr. Wilson is passionate about breaking barriers and creating opportunities for those who identify with the intersectionality of marginalization and minorization, emphasizing equity and access to opportunities. She intentionally creates inclusive spaces where all voices can be heard and all people are empowered to take action that leads to positive change. As an educator, her thought leadership, ability to have tough yet necessary conversations, and attentive diligence contribute to her ability to dig deep into complex challenges and tell stories that matter.

Inspired by Dr. Wilson's story, let's dive deeper into her Leadership Type: The Trailblazer.

Brief Description of The Trailblazer

Trailblazers are seekers. They are driven by what could be rather than what currently is. They are the fearless adventurers at the frontier of the unknown, forming paths where others see dead ends and turning the impossible into the possible.

Internal Motivation of The Trailblazer

The Trailblazer's strongest internal motivation is possibility, or to lead the way and inspire others to follow them in creating a new, better reality. They pioneer new paths, break barriers, and set the course for others to follow. The Trailblazer's words, decisions, and actions can also be influenced by expression and liberation, the internal motivations of their adjacent Leadership Types (The Innovator and The Catalyst).

The greatest fear of The Trailblazer is stagnation, which in a leadership context refers to a lack of growth, progress, or development. Stagnation is characterized by a state of complacency, which goes directly against The Trailblazer's desire to push forward and explore new territories.

An energizing force or amplifier for The Trailblazer is simplicity, the internal motivation of their opposite Type on the SLE, The Pathfinder. For The Trailblazer, this opposing motivation can expand their thinking and be an opportunity for growth because their urge to forge new directions can find grounding in The Pathfinder's more structured approach. The simplicity of The Pathfinder can influence a clearer roadmap, bringing stability to The Trailblazer's more spontaneous journey.

Greatest External Power of The Trailblazer

The Trailblazer's greatest external power is to awaken by challenging conventions and pioneering new paths for themselves and others. They promote and pursue possibilities, encouraging experimentation along the way.

How The Trailblazer Best Communicates & Relates

The Trailblazer empowers ownership and action in others. They encourage risk-taking, curiosity, and stepping out of comfort zones to take on new challenges, and they value unconventional wisdom.

To best communicate with others, here is what The Trailblazer does:

- ✓ Rallies others around possibilities and the potential of unexplored ideas
- ✓ Promotes unconventional thinking and encourages exploration
- ✓ Facilitates open-minded discussions to foster fresh and diverse feedback
- ✓ Compels others toward uncharted possibilities

To best relate to others, here is what The Trailblazer does:

- ✓ Forges connections based on shared enthusiasm for groundbreaking ideas
- ✓ Stokes passion for unprecedented ventures or endeavors

- ✓ Leads brainstorming sessions that pioneer new paths
- ✓ Forms partnerships centered on mutual discovery and adventurous pursuits

Key Leadership Behaviors of The Trailblazer

The Trailblazer embodies an ambitious, exploratory, and potential-pursuing approach to leadership. They inspire others by pursuing new frontiers, and they encourage a culture of fearless pursuit of what is next and what is possible. They are transparent about challenges and learning from risks, maintaining an unwavering commitment to exploration.

When it comes to solving problems, The Trailblazer approaches them with a creative and pioneering mindset, breaking down barriers that hinder innovation or progress, applying out-of-the-box thinking to develop unique solutions, and leveraging cross-disciplinary insights for holistic problem-solving. They overcome obstacles with their adaptability and by embracing challenges as opportunities, using stress as fuel for change and action, and they maintain an adaptable, growth-oriented mindset while prioritizing progress over perfection.

To inform their decision-making, The Trailblazer considers the range of options and potential impact, weighing the benefits of innovative solutions over traditional ones. They make choices that support progress and change and are adept at balancing calculated risks with strategic foresight.

In tandem with this foresight, The Trailblazer shapes spaces by staying focused on what is ahead, looking toward the future with an adventurous spirit. They emphasize and create opportunities to learn from failures and celebrate breakthroughs. To help mitigate bias and remove barriers for others, The Trailblazer creates pathways for unconventional ideas to be heard, advocating for diversity in thought and approach. They actively seek to break down preconceptions that limit potential.

These combined traits allow The Trailblazer to excel in dynamic, fast-paced environments. They can drive growth in professions, industries, and sectors that are ripe for transformation, and they have the potential to significantly influence and impact fields in which innovation is the key to advancement.

Why the World Needs More Trailblazers

- To propel others forward by embracing new possibilities
- To demonstrate that boundaries are meant to be pushed
- To inspire others to reach for a better future
- To act as an agent for change and forward progress

Calls to Action If You Are a Trailblazer

As a Trailblazer Leadership Type, your leadership path is marked by pioneering achievements. You can catalyze environments conducive to progress and innovation. You have a unique opportunity to galvanize those around you to consistently challenge the norm, propelling the entire team or organization toward unparalleled growth and triumph. Here are some specific calls to action and ways you can realize your full leadership potential as a Trailblazer:

→ Pioneer "Frontier Initiatives"
As a leader, recognize your intrinsic drive to continuously innovate. Prioritize and integrate initiatives that focus on taking risks and venturing into unexplored domains. These initiatives should champion groundbreaking ideas and nurture creativity. Here is how to execute them:
- Determine potential areas in your organization or field that beckon innovation.
- Designate sufficient resources—be it time, funds, or team members—for these Frontier Initiatives.
- Grant yourself the freedom and autonomy to steer these projects, allowing your Trailblazing spirit to flourish.
- Once you identify a key initiative, secure a budget and a team that you have the authority to leverage.

→ Launch a "Leadership through Innovation Mentorship Scheme"

Your innate ability to pioneer and inspire can be a guiding light for emerging Trailblazers on your team. Channel this by mentoring individuals with a flair for originality, helping them realize their potential, and fostering a culture of continuous innovation. Here is how to execute this:
- Spot team members who display a knack for inventive thinking and an eagerness to evolve.
- Engage with these individuals on a mentorship journey by participating in regular interactions and feedback loops.
- Motivate your mentees to embark on their own Trailblazing projects, offering your guidance throughout.
- Publicize and celebrate the accomplishments of this mentorship scheme, reinforcing the value of innovation within your team's culture.

→ Embark on a "Societal Trend Analysis"

Understanding and anticipating macro societal trends is essential for driving innovation, staying ahead of the curve, and positioning your organization for long-term success. Here is how to execute this:
- Commission or conduct a research study on macro societal trends.
- Engage in open-ended brainstorms to explore how your industry can adapt and grow alongside these evolving dynamics.

Trailblazers You Should Know

Jackie Robinson epitomizes The Trailblazer leader. Breaking the color barrier in Major League Baseball in 1947, Robinson was a skilled athlete and a courageous pioneer who ventured into uncharted territories. His journey was marked by challenging deep-rooted racial prejudices and societal norms, and his resilience and determination in the face of hostility and discrimination transformed the landscape of American sports and society at large.

A defining moment in Robinson's Trailblazing journey occurred on April 15, 1947, when he debuted for the Brooklyn Dodgers, becoming the first African American to play in Major League Baseball in the modern era. This event was not just about playing a game; it was a significant step in challenging and changing the segregated world of professional sports in America. Robinson's presence on the field was a powerful statement against racial segregation and discrimination. Throughout his career, his excellence in the game and his dignified conduct in the face of constant racism served to open the doors for countless other athletes of color. Robinson's legacy extends far beyond baseball; Robinson is remembered as a symbol of courage and perseverance, a true Trailblazer who showed that boundaries are meant to be pushed and new possibilities embraced for a more inclusive future.

Another great example of The Trailblazer Leadership Type is **Parmesh Shahani**. He stands as a quintessential Trailblazer, his career defined by a relentless pursuit of what could be, particularly in the realms of business, culture, and LGBTQIA+ advocacy in India. At the helm of the Godrej India Culture Lab, Shahani has been pivotal in creating an interdisciplinary platform that not only challenges conventional boundaries but also cultivates an ecosystem where innovation thrives. His commitment to inclusivity and diversity extends beyond mere advocacy, manifesting in tangible initiatives that bridge the divide between corporate India and the LGBTQIA+ community. Shahani's ability to envision and execute groundbreaking projects highlights his intrinsic Trailblazing qualities—fearlessness in the face of societal norms, agility in navigating complex cultural landscapes, and an unwavering belief in the power of experimentation and pioneering new paths.

A defining moment for Shahani as a Trailblazer was the launch of the "Queeristan" initiative, a comprehensive program aimed at transforming corporate India's approach to LGBTQIA+ inclusivity. This initiative not only provided a blueprint for organizations to create more welcoming and supportive environments for LGBTQIA+ employees but also set a new standard for corporate responsibility in India. By leveraging his influential position and extensive network, Shahani was able to encourage significant policy changes and foster a culture of acceptance and respect within some of India's most conservative institutions. This pivotal movement was a testament to Shahani's ability to turn the impossible into the possible, breaking down long-standing barriers and opening new horizons of possibility for diversity and inclusion. Through Queeristan, Shahani both advocated for change and actively blazed a trail for others to follow, embodying the essence of a Trailblazer leader by exploring uncharted territories with courage and conviction.

Other examples of leaders who embody The Trailblazer Leadership Type include poet **Gwendolyn Brooks**, celebrated for her profound literary contributions and historic achievement as the first Black author to win the Pulitzer Prize; **Alice Coachman**, who broke barriers as the first African American woman to win an Olympic Gold Medal in 1948, paving the way for future generations of athletes; **Stacey Abrams**, recognized for her groundbreaking roles as the first female minority leader in the Georgia General Assembly and the first Black woman to be a major party's gubernatorial candidate in the United States; **Wangari Maathai**, a formidable social, environmental, and political activist and the first African woman to receive the Nobel Peace Prize, for her contribution to sustainable development, democracy, and peace; **Sally Ride**, who etched her name in history as the first American woman to fly in space, inspiring countless others to reach for the stars; and **Cory Witherill**, who made history as the first Native American to compete in the Indianapolis 500, demonstrating exceptional courage and determination in the highly competitive world of motorsports.

CATALYST

Catalysts are forces for change. They incite urgent action and disruption, setting the stage for transformation. They challenge others to embrace change and play a pivotal role in fostering opportunities for growth.

Motivation
Liberation through freedom and empowerment for others

Motto
"Disrupt norms"

Promise
To transform current paradigms

Fear
Inertia

Tone of Voice
- Dynamic
- Disruptive
- Transformative
- Stimulating
- Provocative

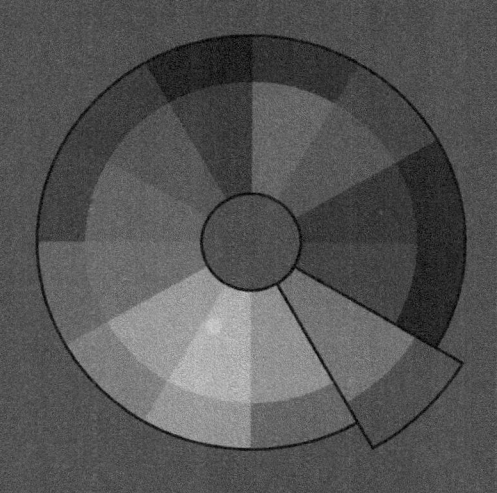

Power
To awaken
- Activating potential
- Enhancing self-assurance
- Championing disruption
- Provoking critical thought

Influences
Enjoyment and Possibility
These motivations of The Ignitor and The Trailblazer influence The Catalyst's thoughts and actions.

Amplifier
Stability
Combined with this internal motivation of The Navigator, Catalysts can expand their thinking and find opportunities for growth.

MEET THE CATALYST

What is this moment requiring of you as a leader?

~Wayne Robinson, senior director of global talent at Moderna

Wayne Robinson is a dynamic talent transformer, an advocate of empowerment, a successful entrepreneur, and an award-winning veteran who crafts paths that awaken potential and fuel purpose-driven leaders and endeavors. He is the quintessential Catalyst.

In his pivotal role as senior director of global talent at Moderna, Robinson directs the brightest minds to pioneer revolutionary healthcare solutions, aiming to elevate global well-being. His visionary leadership is instrumental in cultivating industry leaders whose innovative work in developing transformative medicines is poised to redefine the benchmarks of medical innovation and set new standards of excellence in global health.

In his previous positions at Deloitte and Google, Robinson's roles were essential in establishing two premier leadership institutes: the Deloitte Resilience Academy and The Google School for Leaders. He galvanized the executive echelon for these world-class organizations, fostering strategic and adaptive mindsets to navigate global complexities. These transformative sessions went beyond mere skill enhancement to redefine leadership excellence and establish a benchmark for leadership development across the corporate landscape.

Robinson's approach to strategic leadership was developed throughout his twenty-six years of active military service, four of which he spent serving as a command sergeant, and his near decade of supporting veterans in the years to follow. He led the US Army as a command sergeant for Joint Special Operations and was awarded the Order of Saint Barbara and six Meritorious Service Medals for his indomitable spirit and integrity-driven focus.

Robinson's experience inspired the founding of Vets in STEM, which set a benchmark in facilitating veterans' transitions into civilian life, particularly in the fields of science, technology, engineering, and mathematics. His strategic vision and drive have steered the nonprofit to target the ambitious goal of guiding one hundred thousand service members on their journey to STEM-related careers, thereby addressing critical skill gaps and enriching the workforce with the unique perspectives of veterans.

Further elevating his advocacy, as president and CEO of Student Veterans of America, Robinson initiated the Million Records Project. This transformative program not only proved veterans' commendable graduation rates but also revolutionized educational benefits by significantly expanding the GI Bill to encompass the dependents of fallen service members. It also helped craft the Forever GI Bill, which provides benefits for five hundred thousand additional veterans each year and allows for an extra year of education for those pursuing STEM fields.

With his unique blend of education and experience, Robinson embodies the transformation that is driving change and shaping the future of empowerment, innovation, and integrity-driven leadership.

Inspired by Robinson's story, let's dive deeper into his Leadership Type: The Catalyst.

Brief Description of The Catalyst

Catalysts are forces for change. They incite urgent action and disruption, setting the stage for transformation. They challenge others to embrace change and play a pivotal role in fostering opportunities for growth.

Internal Motivation of The Catalyst

The Catalyst's strongest internal motivation is liberation, or to free and empower others. They seek unconventional approaches to spark innovation and progress for the good of all. The Catalyst's words, decisions, and actions can also be influenced by enjoyment and possibility, the internal motivations of their adjacent Leadership Types (The Ignitor and The Trailblazer).

The greatest fear of The Catalyst is inertia, which in a leadership context refers to a resistance to change and a lack of momentum. Inertia inhibits forward motion, stifling The Catalyst's ability to drive meaningful transformation.

An energizing force or amplifier for The Catalyst is stability, the internal motivation of their opposite Type on the SLE, The Navigator. For The Catalyst, this opposing motivation can expand their thinking and be an opportunity for growth because, through transformative energies, they can gain momentum from The Navigator's steady push. The Navigator's stability can offer The Catalyst a pace, ensuring that their awakenings are timely and impactful.

Greatest External Power of The Catalyst

The Catalyst's greatest external power is to awaken by activating potential in others. They provoke critical thought, enhance self-assurance, and champion disruption.

How The Catalyst Best Communicates & Relates

The Catalyst challenges others to think bigger and be bigger, encouraging bold actions. They empower others to take initiative and make decisions, promoting adaptability and encouraging others to embrace change.

To best communicate with others, here is what The Catalyst does:

- ✔ Encourages critical conversations to initiate change
- ✔ Provokes new perspectives with challenging questions
- ✔ Passionately articulates ideas for transformation
- ✔ Uses vibrant language to engage and motivate action

To best relate to others, here is what The Catalyst does:

- ✔ Motivates others to embrace broad thinking and take bold action

- ✓ Enhances self-assurance, empowering individuals to embrace and lead transformative change
- ✓ Promotes disruptive thinking in collaborative endeavors
- ✓ Galvanizes changemakers committed to substantial progress

Key Leadership Behaviors of The Catalyst

The Catalyst embodies inspirational, transformational leadership. They lead by example with their boldness and adaptability, they are transparent about challenges and the need for change, and they champion the empowerment of every team or community member.

When it comes to solving problems and overcoming obstacles, The Catalyst approaches problems with a transformative mindset, encouraging innovative thinking and challenging their team to think beyond unorthodox solutions and traditional methods. They have a unique ability to break down complex issues into opportunities for improvement, and they welcome obstacles as possibilities for transformation. They see any challenge as an opportunity for a breakthrough, and they are proactive and willing to pivot and change course to sustain momentum.

To inform their decision-making, The Catalyst considers the long-term implications, possibilities, and greatest potential for change. They prioritize initiatives that empower and liberate teams and stakeholders, and they are willing to take risks to do so.

In tandem with this willingness to take risks, The Catalyst shapes spaces by empowering others to consider alternatives, encouraging a culture of change and adaptation, and consistently demonstrating the value of freedom and the challenging of norms. The Catalyst actively seeks to dismantle biases and barriers experienced by others. They do this by promoting diversity of thought to avoid echo chambers and through challenging their own assumptions and encouraging others to do the same. They target the disruption of systemic barriers, leading initiatives for equal opportunity.

These combined traits allow The Catalyst to excel in environments that are dynamic and open to change. They thrive where innovation and disruption are needed, and they have the potential to make the most impact in settings that are adaptable and growth-oriented.

Why the World Needs More Catalysts

- To drive the change necessary for growth and impact
- To inspire and lead the charge toward a more empowered future
- To challenge outdated systems and pave the way for new paradigms
- To ensure that growth and liberation are at the forefront of development

Calls to Action If You Are a Catalyst

As a Catalyst Leadership Type, you can best channel your passion and energy by grounding your innovative spirit in structured, impactful approaches. This strategic balance ensures that your leadership catalyzes transformative shifts that resonate across your team and the organization, enabling you to "steer the ship" in ever-shifting waters. Here are some specific calls to action and ways you can realize your full leadership potential as a Catalyst:

→ Organize Periodic "Disruption Days"
As a Catalyst leader, it is crucial to set aside specific times to intentionally question and challenge the status quo. Establish recurring Disruption Days that focus on groundbreaking brainstorming and foster a spirit of creative dissent. Here is how to lead the charge:
- Set up quarterly Disruption Days on your team's calendar.

- Craft an agenda with activities tailored to spark innovative thinking, such as immersive brainstorming sessions, hackathons, or guest lectures from renowned disruptors in the industry.
- Cultivate an open-minded atmosphere where every proposal, regardless of its audacity, receives thoughtful consideration.
- After each session, highlight and prioritize standout ideas, then delegate teams or individuals to draft a roadmap for execution.

→ Foster a "Safe to Fail" Mindset

Embrace the idea that not every novel venture will pan out. To genuinely innovate, there is an inherent risk of missteps. As a leader, it is your role to instill a culture that views these risks not as potential pitfalls but as opportunities for growth. Here is how to lead the charge:

- Continuously emphasize the merits of taking thoughtful risks and the invaluable insights derived from missteps.
- Applaud both the triumphs and the daring endeavors, recognizing that even if they do not always lead to immediate success, they lay the foundation for future breakthroughs.
- Dedicate time in review sessions for teams to present projects or ideas that did not go as planned, emphasizing the lessons and potential pivots.
- Initiate a feedback mechanism that underscores constructive feedback, ensuring everyone learns and evolves from their endeavors.

→ Prioritize regular recharging by embracing activities to re-energize yourself. This self-care is essential for sustaining the energy needed for impactful leadership and transformative change. Here are some ideas:

- Reflect on your past successes and accomplishments to boost your confidence and motivation to tackle new challenges.

- Adopt a daily meditation routine. There is no wrong way to meditate, and a shorter routine is better than no routine at all.
- Engage in creative activities such as writing, painting, cooking, playing an instrument, or listening to music to refresh yourself and stimulate new ideas.
- Take a designated technology break during the day or set limits to control your technology usage.

Catalysts You Should Know

Marsha P. Johnson stands as a quintessential Catalyst leader. Her relentless advocacy for LGBTQIA+ rights demonstrates her dynamic force for change. Johnson saw opportunities for transformation in a society that was deeply discriminatory toward LGBTQIA+ individuals. Her life was a testament to challenging the status quo and inspiring others to embrace new possibilities for equality and liberation.

A defining moment of Johnson's activism was her involvement in the Stonewall uprising of 1969. The uprising, a series of spontaneous demonstrations against a police raid at the Stonewall Inn in Greenwich Village, became a pivotal event in the fight for LGBTQIA+ rights. Johnson's participation was not just about being present but about being a visible and vocal advocate for change, embodying The Catalyst's spirit of fearlessness and empowerment. Her actions during and after Stonewall sparked a movement that played a pivotal role in fostering opportunities for growth and acceptance within society. Johnson's legacy continues to inspire activists and advocates, demonstrating her profound impact as a leader who constantly sought to awaken potential and drive adaptation in the pursuit of freedom and empowerment for others.

Another great example of The Catalyst Leadership Type is **Luvvie Ajayi Jones,** a four-time *New York Times* best-selling author, award-winning speaker, renowned podcaster, and innovative founder. As the CEO and CCO of Awe Luv Media, Ajayi Jones combines her unique blend of humor and honesty to embolden underrepresented voices and reshape our collective history. Her TED talk "Get Comfortable with Being Uncomfortable" is a powerful call for courage and has achieved global recognition. It has garnered over thirteen million views, been translated into twenty-three languages, and ranks in the top 1 percent of all-time TED Talks.

As a renowned best-selling author, Ajayi Jones has written many books, including *Professional Troublemaker: The Fear-Fighter Manual*, *Rising Troublemaker: A Fear-Fighter Manual for Teens*, *I'm Judging You: The Do-Better Manual*, and the children's book *Little Troublemaker Makes a Mess*. These books showcase her deep conviction in the power of the written word. Her ability to extend storytelling beyond the page inspires a movement of authenticity and cultivates a vibrant community among her millions of followers. Moreover, she serves as a Catalyst for aspiring authors through her recently founded program called The Book Academy. Committed to empowering voices on the margins, The Academy guides these authors from sparking an idea, to writing their truth, to enjoying publication. This innovative storytelling platform ensures that unique narratives are nurtured, celebrated, and shared, enriching our collective consciousness for generations to come.

Ajayi Jones transcends boundaries, bridging cultures and uniting people worldwide. As a transformative leader, she both sparks change and inspires collective action, creating opportunities for diverse truths to be shared. In doing so, she is paving the way for a future fueled by courage, strengthened by community, and deeply committed to inclusion.

Other examples of leaders who embody The Catalyst Leadership Type include **Greta Thunberg**, a Swedish environmental activist whose fearless advocacy for urgent action on climate change has inspired a global youth movement and reshaped public discourse on environmental policies; **X González**, known for their activism in the wake of the Parkland school shooting, for becoming a central figure in the push for gun control in the United States and sparking nationwide debates on gun laws and school safety; **Megan Rapinoe**, an elite athlete who uses her platform to champion LGBTQIA+ rights, racial equality, and gender and pay equity, embodying the spirit of activism within and beyond the sports world; **Alok Vaid-Menon,** a gender nonconforming writer and performance artist who challenges societal norms and advocates for gender inclusivity and queer rights, driving critical discussions on identity and expression; **Hamdi Ulukaya,** founder of Chobani, who has revolutionized the yogurt industry, set new standards for corporate responsibility toward refugees and workers' rights, and advocates for a more humane and inclusive business model; **Stephanie Byers,** a groundbreaking figure as the first openly transgender Native American elected official, promoting visibility and advancing rights for transgender and Indigenous communities; and **Joshua Tenorio,** Lieutenant Governor of Guam and an advocate for LGBTQIA+ rights, representing a significant step forward in the community's visibility and leadership in political spheres.

CATALYST

IGNITOR

Ignitors are the spark. They create vibrant environments that foster positive experiences, and their infectious energy and enthusiasm uplift those around them with a spirit of fulfillment and joy.

Motivation
Enjoyment in bringing joy to others

Motto
"Infuse joy"

Promise
To imbue every moment with positivity and energy

Fear
Apathy

Tone of Voice
- Spirited
- Optimistic
- Energetic
- Present
- Welcoming

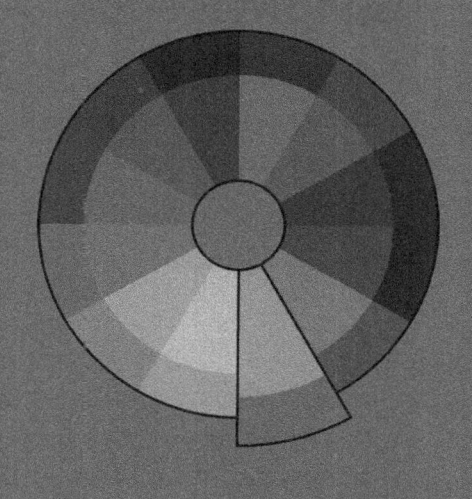

Power
To awaken
- Embracing optimism
- Uplifting others
- Elevating experiences
- Welcoming all

Influences
Relationships and Liberation
These motivations of The Connector and The Catalyst influence The Ignitor's thoughts and actions.

Amplifier
Knowledge
Combined with this internal motivation of The Guide, Ignitors can expand their thinking and find opportunities for growth.

MEET THE IGNITOR

*I focus on the energy.
When people come in, they're immediately in an atmosphere brimming with high energy.*

~Carol Jue, head women's basketball coach at Chapman University

Carol Jue is a groundbreaking figure in the world of collegiate sports. Serving as the first Chinese American head basketball coach in the NCAA, she has built a storied legacy at one of the country's most historic institutions, Chapman University. She is fueled by a lifelong dedication to her players and inspired by all they represent.

With over two decades of head coaching experience at the esteemed Southern California school, Jue has redefined the legacy of the nationally ranked university by propelling its women's basketball program to three hundred wins, nine NCAA Division III playoff berths, and nine 20-win seasons. Under her intentional guidance, the team has also achieved five All-West Region selections, three Academic All-Americans, six Academic All-District honorees, and three Athlete of the Year awards from the Southern California Intercollegiate Athletic Conference (SCIAC). Jue's crowning achievement came in the 2017–2018 season when she led the team to their first-ever SCIAC Tournament title. Jue's dynamic leadership and spirited coaching prowess have garnered her the accolade of SCIAC Coaching Staff of the Year for three consecutive years.

For Jue, basketball transcends sport; it acts as a catalyst for personal development and inspiration. And she is committed to using her platform to uplift others both on and off the court. Determined to expand access to sports for women worldwide, Jue uses her voice in public speaking, articles, and media interviews to emphasize the importance of life skills and overcoming fears.

As a Trailblazer, Jue empowers women to think positively, guiding them through personal growth and inspiring them to chase their dreams. As a coach, she strikes a balance between developing players to be at their best physically, emotionally, and mentally. At her core, she is dedicated to preparing young women for life beyond the basketball court, helping them discover their true identities and nurturing a strong sense of teamwork. A champion of representation, Jue underscores the significance of ethics and character in all aspects of life.

Jue holds a bachelor's degree in economics and accounting from Claremont McKenna College. She was an accomplished student-athlete and was eventually named MVP and First Team All SCIAC. Her basketball career, which began at Montebello High, was recognized with an induction into the Montebello High Hall of Fame, as an individual in 2011 and as part of a team in 2015.

Seeing challenges and adversity as chances to excel and stand for something greater than ourselves, Jue is committed to empowering others and is a dedicated representative of her family and community. Residing in Tustin, California, with her husband, Kevin, and sons, Ryley and Carson, Jue takes pride in being a Trailblazing first-generation American, paving the way for fellow Chinese Americans around the world.

Inspired by Jue's story, let's dive deeper into her Leadership Type: The Ignitor.

Brief Description of The Ignitor

Ignitors are the spark. They create vibrant environments that foster positive experiences, and their infectious energy and enthusiasm uplift those around them with a spirit of fulfillment and joy.

Internal Motivation of The Ignitor

The Ignitor's strongest internal motivation is enjoyment, or bringing joy to others. They infuse positivity and enthusiasm into what they do while cultivating a vibrant and uplifting environment for those around them. The Ignitor's words, decisions, and actions can also be influenced by relationships and liberation, the internal motivations of their adjacent Leadership Types (The Connector and The Catalyst).

The greatest fear of The Ignitor is apathy, which in a leadership context refers to a state of disinterest, indifference, or lack of motivation among team members or an organization. Apathy can threaten The Ignitor's engagement and extinguish their enthusiasm.

An energizing force, or amplifier for The Ignitor is knowledge, the internal motivation of their opposite Type on the SLE, The Guide. For The Ignitor, this opposing motivation can expand their thinking and be an opportunity for growth because their radiance can find resonance in The Guide's wisdom. The Guide's sense of understanding can provide substance to The Ignitor's joy, balancing exhilaration with enlightenment.

Greatest External Power of The Ignitor

The Ignitor's greatest external power is to awaken by embracing optimism. By welcoming all and uplifting others, they elevate experiences.

How The Ignitor Best Communicates & Relates

The Ignitor creates a vibrant, high-energy atmosphere in which they nurture potential and empowerment. They create a dynamic environment that helps others build confidence through positive reinforcement and celebrating unique contributions.

To best communicate with others, here is what The Ignitor does:

- ✔ Uses positive and energizing language
- ✔ Shares enthusiasm to encourage others
- ✔ Spreads optimism and joy in interactions
- ✔ Keeps spirits high

To best relate to others, here is what The Ignitor does:

- ✔ Fosters a welcoming and warm environment
- ✔ Builds connections through shared positive experiences
- ✔ Encourages open, optimistic, and supportive dialogue
- ✔ Celebrates the individuality and passion of each person

Key Leadership Behaviors of The Ignitor

The Ignitor leads with heart, displaying energetic and joyful leadership. They keep the team's spirits high, especially during tough times, by consistently celebrating unique contributions, nurturing possibilities, and using positive reinforcement.

When it comes to solving problems, The Ignitor does so with optimism and creative thinking. They frame challenges as opportunities for teams to come together, energizing team members to find positive solutions, and they create a safe space for brainstorming and playful problem-solving. To overcome obstacles, The Ignitor maintains perspective, remains optimistic, and celebrates small wins.

To inform their decision-making, The Ignitor weighs the options against the potential for joy and positivity in outcomes, considering the impact on team morale and energy. They seek options that are likely to deliver enjoyment and satisfaction, balancing practicality with the potential to inspire and energize.

In tandem with this positive and inspirational energy, The Ignitor shapes spaces by proactively promoting joy and enthusiasm, leading by example with a vivacious and spirited demeanor. They infuse fun when and where appropriate, prioritizing happiness to boost engagement, satisfaction, and morale. When they encounter bias and barriers, The Ignitor overcomes them by both cultivating a work environment where joy is accessible to everyone and actively working against the dampening effect of negative biases. They encourage a culture in which different sources of happiness are recognized and respected, championing policies and practices that promote positive engagement for all.

These combined traits allow The Ignitor to excel in roles that demand vibrancy and the ability to energize. They fit well in creative industries and spaces and thrive in dynamic environments that benefit from transformational experiences.

Why the World Needs More Ignitors

- To inject energy and passion into teams and projects
- To inspire joy and happiness in others
- To combat apathy and disengagement with infectious enthusiasm
- To serve as a model of positivity, leading others to find greater fulfillment

Calls to Action If You Are an Ignitor

As an Ignitor Leadership Type, your unique ability to engage others can make for a brighter workplace, one that can support the mental and emotional health of others. Your gift of infusing joy into even tense situations can dramatically shift team dynamics, boosting adaptability and creativity. By integrating creative techniques into your leadership strategy, you light the path to a more motivated and ultimately successful team. Here are some specific calls to action and ways you can realize your full leadership potential as an Ignitor:

→ Lead "Joyful Jam Sessions"
Take the initiative to harness your potential to elevate team spirits. Craft moments when your vibrant energy can be a beacon for the entire team. Here is how to execute this:
- Slot Joyful Jam Sessions into the team's schedule, preferably as a refreshing start or wrap-up to the workweek.
- Encourage the team to prepare short, light-hearted anecdotes, music, or even a showcase of their unique talents.

- This is not just about having fun; it is about allowing your inner Ignitor to lead in a way that resonates with your strengths while reenergizing the team.

→ Initiate a "Joy Wall" Project:
Leverage your knack for positivity by designating a Joy Wall in the workspace, meaning a space of shared optimism and motivation. Here is how to execute this:
- Identify a visible and accessible area in the office for the Joy Wall. If your team operates remotely, opt for a digital platform that allows interactive collaboration.
- Curate and oversee this space, adding and updating content that embodies positivity.
- Promote it as a go-to spot for team members needing a burst of inspiration or a simple smile.

→ Cultivate Gratitude
Develop a practice of gratitude, both for yourself and for your team. You can execute this by recognizing and appreciating the contributions and value that each team member brings to the table.

Ignitors You Should Know

Lin-Manuel Miranda exemplifies The Ignitor leader. His work in theater demonstrates his unique ability to cultivate confidence, empower action, and enhance environments through his artistic vision. Miranda's infectious energy and enthusiasm have not only uplifted audiences around the world but also sparked a renewed interest in musical theater and American history among a new generation.

A defining moment in Miranda's career as an Ignitor was the creation and debut of *Hamilton*, a musical that blends hip-hop, jazz, and traditional show tunes to tell the story of American Founding Father Alexander Hamilton. This groundbreaking work transcended the boundaries of traditional Broadway theater, attracting a diverse audience and garnering widespread acclaim.

Miranda's approach to *Hamilton*—using vibrant, high-energy music and storytelling to bring history to life—exemplifies his ability to create a joyful, spirited atmosphere that resonates deeply with audiences. His success with the musical and other projects highlights his talent for nurturing possibility and empowerment and fostering a sense of communal joy and engagement, all key traits of an Ignitor leader.

Another great example of The Ignitor Leadership Type is **Michaela Jaé Rodriguez.** Through her groundbreaking achievements and roles, Rodriguez epitomizes the essence of an Ignitor—a Leadership Type characterized by the ability to spark change and inspire others by breaking new ground. Her historic Emmy nomination for a lead acting category not only shattered long-standing barriers within the entertainment industry but also highlighted the depth and diversity of trans narratives that had been overlooked for far too long. Rodriguez's portrayal of Blanca Rodriguez in *Pose* transcended mere acting; it was a powerful assertion of visibility and representation for the transgender community. This moment was not just a personal triumph for Rodriguez but a beacon of progress for trans individuals everywhere, demonstrating her potential to ignite significant social and cultural transformation through the medium of entertainment.

Following her Emmy nomination, Rodriguez's subsequent win at the Golden Globe Awards further cemented her role as an Ignitor. Her victory was more than just an accolade; it was a historic moment that challenged and changed the narrative around transgender talent in Hollywood and beyond. Through her talent, resilience, and visibility, Rodriguez has opened doors and laid the groundwork for future generations of trans actors and actresses, proving that representation matters deeply. Her journey and successes inspire not only those within the LGBTQIA+ community but also allies and advocates for diversity and inclusion across all sectors. Rodriguez's achievements serve as a shining example of how Ignitors lead by example, using their platforms to challenge the status quo and spark meaningful conversations and actions toward a more inclusive society.

Other examples of leaders who embody The Ignitor Leadership Type include **Dwayne "The Rock" Johnson**, a global entertainment superstar known for his charismatic energy, humor, and motivational persona; **Michelle Obama**, the former First Lady of the United States whose continued advocacy work, public speaking, and initiatives on education, health, and women's empowerment have made her a role model and a source of inspiration and joy for many; **Diana Nyad**, a world champion swimmer known for her historic swim from Cuba to Florida and her unyielding spirit and infectious energy in the face of numerous challenges; **Dolly Parton**, a country music icon, an actor, a humanitarian, and a philanthropist who has cemented a legacy of charity and positivity; **Oprah Winfrey**, a media mogul and philanthropist whose influential talk show and charitable endeavors have transformed lives and inspired millions globally; and **Sarah Blakely**, the founder of Spanx, who with her innovative vision and relentless drive has redefined the apparel industry while empowering women around the world to embrace their confidence and achieve their goals.

QUADRANT 3:
THE POWER TO UNITE

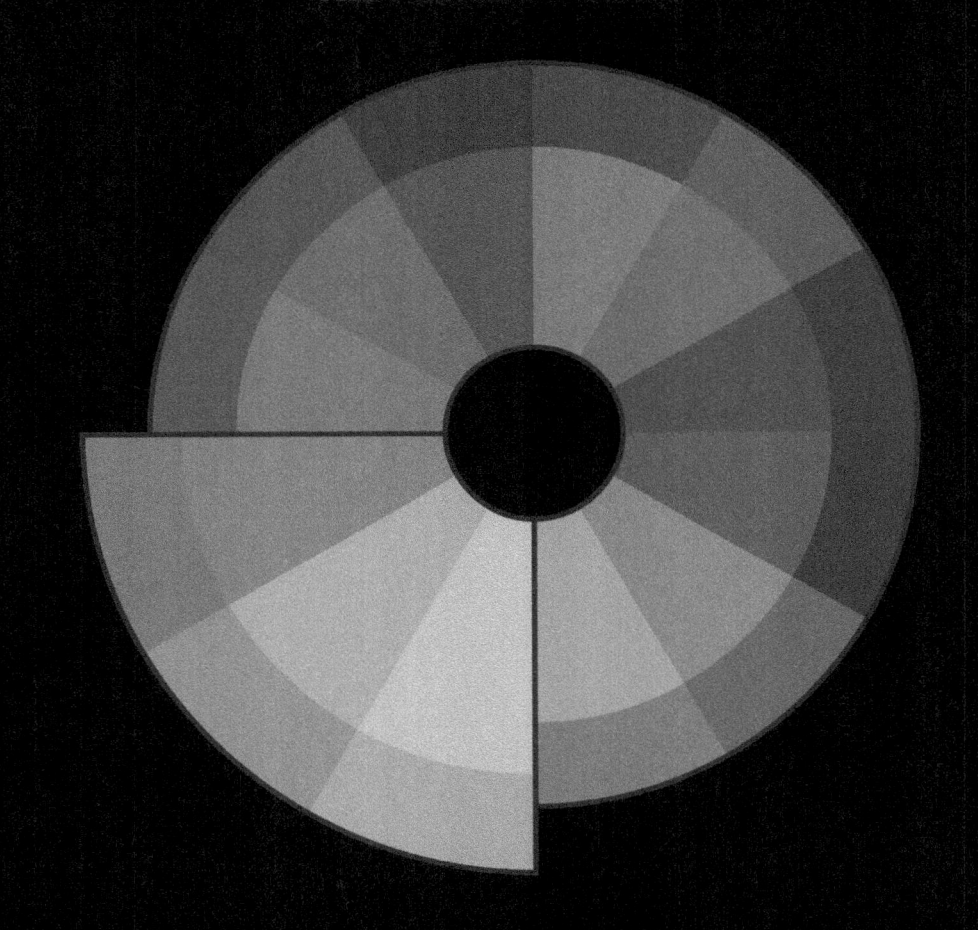

Leaders within the realm of quadrant 3 of the SLE are intrinsically driven by the desire to bring people together, to unite them under shared ideals, and to ensure that everyone feels seen, heard, and valued. They understand that real change, the kind that leaves an indelible mark, often comes from collective efforts rather than isolated endeavors.

In a world where individualism can sometimes overshadow collective well-being, a distinctive set of leaders emerges—those who symbolize unity and togetherness. These are the architects of bonds, the guardians of camaraderie, and the harmonizers of diverse voices. Their focus is not solely on the destination but on ensuring that the journey is undertaken together, with mutual respect and understanding. They know the power of unity in diversity and harness it to create a more inclusive, compassionate world. Representing this power to unite, we find The Connector, The Protector, and The Champion.

The Connector recognizes the inherent strength in unity and works tirelessly to link people, ideas, and communities. They understand that true belonging does not stem from mere association but from deep-rooted connections.

The Protector is the pillar of support that everyone can lean on. They constantly look out for those who might need assistance, ensuring they have the necessary resources and emotional support to thrive.

The Champion is a force to be reckoned with. They not only stand up for justice but actively challenge prevailing notions that perpetuate inequity. Their mission is to elevate the voices that often go unheard, ensuring that justice is not just an ideal but a tangible reality for all.

Together, these leaders are the binding threads that bring teams, organizations, and communities together, emphasizing unity, shared purpose, and mutual growth.

Connector

Connectors are relationship-builders. They seek to develop outcomes greater than the sum of their parts, and they are able to earn the trust of others because of their natural relatability and likability.

Motivation
Relationships through making connections among people

Motto
"Build bonds"

Promise
To foster meaningful and collaborative networks

Fear
Isolation

Tone of Voice
- Active
- Committed
- Magnetic
- Relational
- Engaging

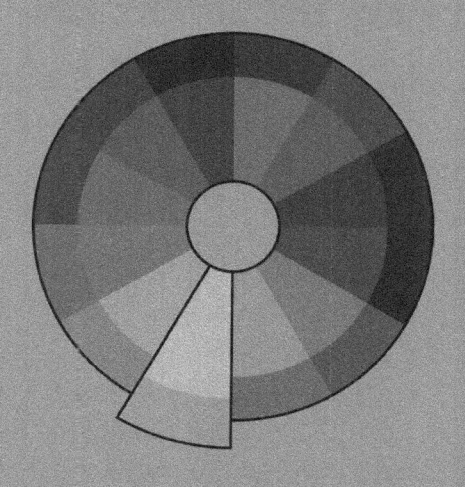

Power
To unite
- Building communities
- Encouraging collaboration
- Engaging others
- Fostering mutuality

Influences
Altruism and Enjoyment
These motivations of The Protector and The Ignitor influence The Connector's thoughts and actions.

Amplifier
Realization
Combined with this internal motivation of The Visionary, Connectors can expand their thinking and find opportunities for growth.

MEET THE CONNECTOR

I bring people together because I see something beyond what they can see. I put people in a room with a purpose.

~Corinne Milien, founder and CEO of WRK

Corinne Milien is a steadfast servant leader with numerous experiences focusing on solutions to help others overcome workforce challenges and advance equal access to professional development.

A two-time founder and CEO with over ten years of experience in the sports and entertainment industry, Milien leverages her expertise in human capital management to optimize organizational performance. As the leader of WRK, she delivers innovative and tailored people solutions to drive personal and professional success for her clients.

In parallel to this role, Milien serves as the cofounder and executive director of The Winning Edge Leadership Academy, a 501(c)(3) organization empowering and creating a community of influence for the next generation of women and minorities in the sports and entertainment industry.

Milien's past experiences in the sports industry include serving as managing director for the Pro Sports Assembly, where she led the membership, partnership, and programming efforts to advance the mission of uniting leaders to advance and deliver a fair future for all in the professional sports industry, including teams, leagues, unions, and venues. Prior to that, Milien was a graduate assistant for the legendary Coach Pat Summitt of The University of Tennessee and as an events supervisor for ESPN. At the latter, she managed several of the company's preeminently owned and operated athletic contests and events.

Milien has been recognized with multiple awards and honors for her leadership and social impact, including being selected as a participant in the adidas Cultivate & B.L.O.O.M. accelerator program, being selected as a member of the National Sports Forum Business of Diversity in Sports and Entertainment, and being named the NYU SPS Sports Business Society Ambassador of the Year.

Milien is a veteran, having served honorably in the US Air Force before attending the United States Air Force Academy. She holds a bachelor's degree from Bemidji State University and a master's degree from the University of Tennessee, both in sports management.

As the proud daughter of Haitian immigrants, Milien stays true to her roots and maintains a relentless work ethic in all endeavors, consistently devoting her infectious energy toward doing good and ultimately creating equity and opportunity for others in the workplace and beyond..

Inspired by Milien's story, let's dive deeper into her Leadership Type: The Connector.

Brief Description of The Connector

Connectors are relationship-builders. They seek to develop outcomes greater than the sum of their parts, and they are able to earn the trust of others because of their natural relatability and likability.

Internal Motivation of The Connector

The Connector's strongest internal motivation is relationships, or making connections among people. The Connector's words, decisions, and actions can also be influenced by altruism and enjoyment, the internal motivations of their adjacent Leadership Types (The Protector and The Ignitor).

The greatest fear of The Connector is isolation, which in a leadership context refers to the state of being disconnected, detached, or socially withdrawn from others. Isolation diminishes The Connector's opportunities to collaborate, negatively impacting their morale and limiting their access to valuable network resources.

An energizing force, or amplifier for The Connector is realization, the internal motivation of their opposite Type on the SLE,

The Visionary. For The Connector, this opposing motivation can expand their thinking and be an opportunity for growth because the expansive networks of The Connector can be inspired by The Visionary's dreams. The Visionary's sense of realization can help fill The Connector's connections with purpose, ensuring that bonds are both strong and forward-thinking.

Greatest External Power of The Connector

The Connector's greatest external power is to unite by engaging with others and seeking to develop outcomes greater than the sum of their parts. In the workplace (and in life), this looks like building communities, encouraging collaboration, and fostering mutuality. Connectors bridge gaps and forge strong networks for collective success.

How The Connector Best Communicates & Relates

The Connector establishes a shared purpose, promotes a collaborative environment, and ensures harmony. They enhance outcomes by finding common ground, building consensus, and identifying synergies between people and groups.

To best communicate with others, here is what The Connector does:

- ✔ Facilitates open dialogue to foster meaningful connections
- ✔ Listens actively and acknowledges others' ideas
- ✔ Encourages collaborative discussions to build consensus
- ✔ Initiates active conversations to strengthen relationships and collaboration

To best relate to others, here is what The Connector does:

- ✔ Builds relationships based on mutual respect
- ✔ Maintains consistent and caring communication
- ✔ Balances professional and personal interactions
- ✔ Creates an engaging atmosphere

Key Leadership Behaviors of The Connector

The Connector is all about collaboration. They establish a shared purpose and promote an environment of teamwork and unity, and they can enhance outcomes through identifying synergies.

When it comes to solving problems, The Connector does so by applying a multifaceted approach to achieve the most sustainable results. They gather diverse perspectives through networking and co-create solutions with the team, valuing each team member's input. The Connector overcomes obstacles by seeking support from personal and professional networks, embracing community as a source of comfort and solutions. They share challenges to find collective solutions.

To inform their decision-making, The Connector considers the impact of various options on team dynamics, balancing individual needs with the group's objectives and striving for decisions that benefit all stakeholders. They focus on harmonious and collaborative outcomes.

In tandem with this cooperative mindset, The Connector shapes spaces by promoting a collaborative culture and valuing individual contributions to a group's identity. They celebrate collective achievements and encourage social connections within the team. When they encounter bias and barriers, they overcome them by leading initiatives to create an accepting environment and advocating for inclusive and equitable practices within their organization. They work hard to ensure that every voice is heard and accounted for, dismantling barriers to diversity within the team when they arise.

These combined traits allow The Connector to thrive in collaborative and diverse settings, excelling in roles that require consensus and community-building. They can uniquely influence environments in which relationships are key to success.

Why the World Needs More Connectors

- To bridge cultural, social, and economic divides
- To cultivate robust networks that empower individuals and groups

- To build resilient teams and communities through strong relationships
- To facilitate community cohesion and teamwork

Calls to Action If You Are a Connector

As a Connector Leadership Type, your ability to forge solid relationships, both internally and externally, is invaluable. By actively channeling your Connector powers, your teams can capitalize on a richer tapestry of ideas, expertise, and experiences. This not only sparks innovation but also builds a culture of collective triumph. Here are some specific calls to action and ways you can realize your full leadership potential as a Connector:

→ Host Frequent Networking Events:
As a leader with the gift of connecting, you should regularly initiate networking sessions termed "Connection Hours." These moments should empower your team to exchange their ideas, projects, and expertise, promoting collaboration across different departments. Here is how to implement them:
- Schedule these events either in-person or virtually on a monthly or bimonthly basis.
- Incorporate engaging formats such as speed networking, roundtable discussions, or quick presentation sessions.
- Use your Connector skills to steer these events by introducing participants, highlighting potential synergies, and ensuring inclusive participation. After each session, solicit feedback to refine the format and bolster engagement.

→ Establish a "Connector's Hub" on Your Company's Digital Space
Utilize your unique capability to unify by setting up a dedicated space on the company's intranet or portal. Here, your

team can propose ideas, seek out collaboration partners, or distribute valuable resources. Envision it as an online community board, nurtured by your Connector instincts, to amplify interdepartmental dialogue and teamwork. Here is how to implement one:

- Allocate a specific segment on the company's digital platform titled "Connector's Hub."
- Empower team members to put forth project suggestions, make collaboration invitations, or disseminate their expertise.
- You, as The Connector, can spotlight triumphant collaborations, provide insights on promising partnerships, and disseminate news on upcoming networking events.
- Periodically evaluate the platform's effectiveness, fine-tuning it based on user input and feedback.

→ Build Global Connections

Building a global network of connections is essential to accessing diverse perspectives, facilitating collaboration, navigating cultural complexities, and seizing market opportunities. Here's how to build your global network:

- Reflect on how to establish global connections around causes you care about.
- Explore various channels, associations, or organizations that can facilitate meaningful interactions across the world.

Connectors You Should Know

The late **Cecilia Gentili** embodied the essence of a Connector leader through her extensive work in LGBTQIA+ advocacy and health. Her direct service efforts at various community centers, cofounding of the COIN Clinic, and leadership roles at Gay Men's Health Crisis showcased her commitment to building communities and forging strong networks. By founding Trans Equity Consulting, she further solidified her role in crafting partnerships and advocating for transgender and gender nonbinary rights on large platforms, including challenging biases in mainstream media. Gentili's work exemplifies the power of connection in uniting people and advancing inclusivity.

A defining moment for Gentili as a Connector came during a pivotal town hall meeting aimed at addressing the healthcare disparities being experienced by the transgender community. Faced with a room divided by skepticism, fear, and systemic barriers, Gentili shined brightly as she navigated the tensions with empathy and strategic insight. She facilitated a dialogue that not only bridged the gap between healthcare providers and the transgender community but also led to the establishment of comprehensive care protocols that are sensitive to the unique needs of transgender patients. This moment was a testament to Gentili's ability to bring together diverse groups and foster an environment of understanding and cooperation that would lay the groundwork for lasting change. Through her intuitive understanding of people and her knack for making meaningful connections, Gentili demonstrated that the heart of advocacy is not just in speaking out but in connecting deeply with others to create a collective voice for change.

Another emblematic example of The Connector Leadership Type is **Rigoberta Menchú Tum**. As an Indigenous rights activist from Guatemala, Menchú Tum has dedicated her life to advocating for the rights of Indigenous peoples and promoting social justice globally. Her ability to articulate the struggles and aspirations of Indigenous communities has united people from different walks of life in the fight for human rights. Her work has transcended cultural and national boundaries, making her a global symbol of peace and unity.

A defining moment in Menchú Tum's role as a Connector was her reception of the Nobel Peace Prize in 1992. The award brought international attention to the plight of Guatemala's Indigenous people and the broader struggle for Indigenous rights worldwide. Menchú Tum's Nobel lecture served as a profound call to unity, urging respect for diversity and the empowerment of Indigenous voices. She used this moment in the spotlight to propel her newfound platform to connect diverse movements and catalyze a global conversation about peace, justice, and reconciliation.

Other examples of leaders who embody The Connector Leadership Type include **Bayard Rustin**, an advisor to Martin Luther King Jr. and the chief organizer of the 1963 March on Washington, whose strategic planning and ability to bring together diverse groups for a common cause and build coalitions were vital to the momentum of the civil rights movement in the United States; **Susan Burton**, a social activist and the founder of A New Way of Life, which provides housing and support for formerly incarcerated women and fights for criminal justice reform; **Brené Brown**, a research professor whose books, talks, and workshops have united millions and created communities of empathy and understanding; **Benazir Bhutto**, the first woman to head a democratic government in a majority Muslim nation, and a leader who sought to bridge the gaps between various political, religious, and cultural factions within Pakistan; **Jacinda Ardern**, the Prime Minister of New Zealand, known for her empathetic leadership style, her ability to connect with people across all levels of society, and her fostering of a sense of unity and collective action in times of crisis; and **Dr. Vivek Murthy**, the US Surgeon General, who through his book *Together: The Healing Power of Human Connection in a Sometimes Lonely World* emphasizes the importance of social connections for public health, advocating for a more interconnected and supportive society.

PROTECTOR

Protectors are servant leaders. They prioritize the needs of the people they lead over their own self-interests, and their actions and decisions are driven by what would benefit others as opposed to short-term gains for themselves.

Motivation
Altruism through genuine concern for others

Motto
"Safeguard others"

Promise
To provide support and understanding

Fear
Betrayal

Tone of Voice
- Supportive
- Generous
- Compassionate
- Nurturing
- Empathetic

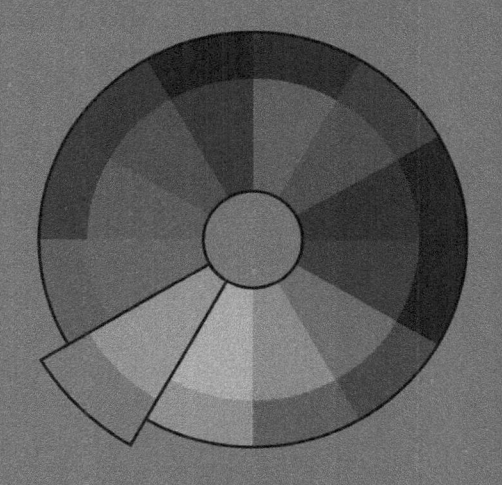

Power
To unite
- Engaging empathetically
- Creating safe spaces
- Prioritizing others
- Providing support

Influences
Relationships and Understanding
These motivations of The Connector and The Champion influence The Protector's thoughts and actions.

Amplifier
Redemption
Combined with this internal motivation of The Legend, Protectors can expand their thinking and find opportunities for growth.

MEET THE PROTECTOR

We often get caught up in structure and fear of sharing knowledge, space, and power, which diminishes people's opportunities and access. If you're in leadership for the right reasons, you know there is space, and, quite frankly, responsibility and competence, in relinquishing some of the power that comes with having a title.

~Allison Feaster, vice president of the Boston Celtics

Allison Feaster is a former professional basketball player, a global citizen, and a changemaker in the sports industry who is highly regarded for her leadership and team-building skills. During her decorated college basketball career, Feaster was the first player in any sport to be honored as Ivy League Player of the Year three times, leading the first-ever NCAA Division I Tournament upset of No. 16 seed Harvard against No. 1 seed Stanford. She was a first-round WNBA draft pick and went on to a seventeen-year professional playing career in the United States, Spain, France, Italy, and Portugal.

Following her retirement from playing in 2016, Feaster joined the NBA's Basketball Operations Management Development program. After serving as the lead of player personnel and coach relations for the NBA G League, she joined the Boston Celtics, where she currently leads player development and organizational growth, impacting both the basketball and business operations of the organization.

Beyond the court, Feaster serves as a co-lead for Boston Celtics United, the team's social justice initiative that she helped conceive after the murder of George Floyd to impact social and racial inequities in Black and Brown communities in Greater Boston. She maintains her role as an active public speaker and a champion of the advancement of women and girls, and she serves as a global advocate for sports, including serving as a Sports Envoy for the US Department of State's Bureau of Educational and Cultural Affairs.

Inspired by Feaster's story, let's dive deeper into her Leadership Type: The Protector.

Brief Description of The Protector

Protectors are servant leaders. They prioritize the needs of the people they lead over their own self-interests, and their actions and decisions are driven by what would benefit others as opposed to short-term gains for themselves.

Internal Motivation of The Protector

The Protector's strongest internal motivation is altruism, or having genuine concern for others. They create stability and foster comfort for those around them. The Protector's words, decisions, and actions can also be influenced by relationships and understanding, the motivations of their adjacent Leadership Types (The Connector and The Champion).

The greatest fear of The Protector is betrayal, which in a leadership context refers to the act of breaking trust or loyalty toward a leader, team, or organization. Protectors know that betrayal damages relationships, undermines unity, and threatens an individual or group's sense of security.

An energizing force or amplifier for The Protector is redemption, the internal motivation of their opposite Type on the SLE, The Legend. For The Protector, this opposing motivation can expand their thinking and be an opportunity for growth because their unifying efforts can be invigorated by The Legend's fervent backing. The Legend can give voice to The Protector's calls, ensuring unity is both heartfelt and empowering.

Greatest External Power of The Protector

The Protector's greatest external power is to unite by prioritizing and engaging with others empathetically. They can create safe, supportive spaces for others.

How The Protector Best Communicates & Relates

The Protector places the well-being of others at the forefront of their leadership. They seek to promote mutual support and morale among others, and they inspire others to consider their broader impact, centered around the emotional and social support of team members.

To best communicate with others, here is what The Protector does:

- ✔ Prioritizes compassionate interactions for a nurturing environment
- ✔ Engages empathetically, deeply understanding individual needs
- ✔ Offers reassurance, fostering safety and well-being
- ✔ Facilitates open and emotionally attuned dialogue

To best relate to others, here is what The Protector does:

- ✔ Shows genuine interest in the lives of others
- ✔ Is consistently approachable and available
- ✔ Establishes trust
- ✔ Promotes an environment of mutual support and loyalty

Key Leadership Behaviors of The Protector

The Protector displays an accessible and supportive style of leadership. They are role models for selflessness and integrity, leading with a sense of duty and a focus on the greater good. They strive to make choices that align with the core values of protection and service, upholding a commitment to the team's welfare in all actions.

When it comes to solving problems, The Protector does so with a mindset of service and support, prioritizing solutions that prioritize people. They seek to address the root causes rather than just the symptoms, and they resolve issues with an emphasis on fairness and protection. They mobilize resources to ensure team members have what they need to succeed. To overcome obstacles, The Protector maintains a calm and composed demeanor, leverages their supportive network as a buffer against stress, and seeks to alleviate pressures.

To inform their decision-making, The Protector considers the input of others who are impacted by the decision and weighs the options against the long-term welfare of both the team and the organization. They prioritize the collective good and seek to protect the interests of all stakeholders, especially the most vulnerable.

In tandem with this selfless mindset, The Protector shapes spaces by championing a culture of service and support centered on a sense of care and consideration for others. They celebrate selflessness and value trust and transparency. When they encounter bias and barriers, they overcome them by actively creating equitable opportunities for all team members, challenging biases and prejudices that threaten team cohesion, and advocating for policies and practices that promote inclusivity. They lead by example in treating all individuals with equal respect.

These combined traits allow The Protector to excel in roles that require nurturing and developing talent, and they thrive in environments where protecting and mentoring are valued. They can have influence in fields that prioritize humanity and the human connection.

Why the World Needs More Protectors

- To fill the critical role of safeguarding others
- To provide a sense of security that enables others to flourish
- To foster trust and loyalty among others
- To guide organizations toward more ethical, human-centric practices

Calls to Action If You Are a Protector

As a Protector Leadership Type, your commitment to standing beside your team members is your greatest strength. You have the unique ability to create an atmosphere in which each individual feels genuinely supported and understood. This nurturing environment strengthens team cohesion and amplifies collective motivation and output. Here are some specific calls to action and ways you can realize your full leadership potential as a Protector:

→ Initiate "All-Hands Support Sessions"
Embrace your role as a Protector by fostering a supportive community within your team. Establish regular All-Hands Support Sessions when everyone can come together to share their challenges and cocreate solutions. Here is how to execute them:
- Designate specific dates for these sessions, ensuring they are consistent and known to all.
- Cultivate a culture of trust and openness, encouraging every team member to voice their concerns without fear.
- Lead these sessions with a collaborative spirit, channeling your inner ally to offer guidance and support.
- Ensure each discussed challenge is revisited in subsequent sessions to track progress and demonstrate your commitment to supporting the team.

→ Launch a "Mentorship Initiative"
Utilize your innate compassion and commitment as a Protector to spearhead a Mentorship Initiative, especially focusing on those who might feel overlooked or underrepresented. Here is how to execute one:
- Pinpoint potential mentees within your team who could greatly benefit from guidance and support.
- Dedicate a portion of your time to mentoring and scheduling regular interactions with your mentee.
- Through this initiative, prioritize fostering relationships across different facets of your team, emphasizing unity and mutual respect.
- Publicly acknowledge the milestones achieved through the mentorship, underlining its significance

in nurturing a collaborative and inclusive team culture.
→ Initiate "ERG Leadership Listening Sessions"
Employee resource groups, or ERGs, are internal communities of individuals within an organization with shared identities and interests. Once you have established ERGs, here are some ways you can engage with and support your ERG leaders:
- Set up listening sessions with the ERG leaders across your organization to understand diverse perspectives and foster inclusivity.
- Gather feedback and solutions to make sure that the ERGs are meeting your employees' expectations in terms of support as well as aligning with the organization's overall DEI priorities.

Protectors You Should Know

Wilma Mankiller's impact is marked by her efforts to protect and enhance the sovereignty of the Cherokee Nation. She worked tirelessly to improve the nation's education, health, and housing. Under her leadership, infant mortality rates decreased, and employment opportunities increased within the Cherokee community. Mankiller's initiatives often involved fostering relationships with the federal government to ensure that treaties were honored and that the rights of her people were protected.

A pivotal moment in Wilma Mankiller's journey as a Protector came in 1985 when she was elected Principal Chief of the Cherokee Nation. Her ascension to this role was not just a personal triumph but a historic milestone for both the Cherokee people and Native Americans broadly. It represented a break from the male-dominated leadership in tribal politics. As Chief, she faced the immense challenge of a community grappling with poverty and health issues. Undeterred, Mankiller implemented community development programs that were rooted in Cherokee traditions while embracing modern solutions. Her leadership led to the revival of a dilapidated Cherokee water system, which not only provided a vital resource but also symbolized the reclamation of autonomy and well-being for her people. This endeavor exemplified her commitment to protecting and empowering her community. Mankiller's legacy is profound. She is remembered for her protective nurturing of her people and her transformative impact on the lives of the Cherokee Nation.

Another emblematic example of The Protector Leadership Type is **Sergio Rodríguez.** He exemplifies the essence of a Protector through his leadership at the Hector and Gloria López Foundation. His unwavering dedication to enhancing the academic and professional prospects of Latino students and faculty is a testament to his altruistic nature and his commitment to creating a more equitable and inclusive society. By prioritizing the needs and well-being of others, especially within underserved communities, Rodríguez has become a beacon of hope and a source of profound support. His approach goes beyond mere philanthropy to nurture potential and empower a community that has been historically marginalized. The foundation's initiatives, from providing scholarships to fostering Latino leadership, reflect a deep understanding of the systemic barriers that impede success and an earnest effort to dismantle them. Rodríguez's leadership is grounded in empathy, generosity, and a genuine concern for the well-being of others, making him a quintessential Protector who seeks to safeguard and uplift those around him.

A defining moment for Rodríguez as a Protector came when he orchestrated a landmark initiative aimed at increasing Latino student graduation rates and ensuring these students had pathways to meaningful leadership roles within academia and beyond. Recognizing the profound impact of representation, Rodríguez led efforts to establish mentorship programs that connect Latino students with Latino leaders and professionals. This initiative was not merely about academic achievement but about fostering a sense of belonging and community, critical elements in nurturing future leaders. Through this and similar initiatives, Rodríguez has created a supportive ecosystem that validates and celebrates Latino heritage, encouraging students to pursue excellence without compromising their identities. His actions underscore The Protector's promise to provide support and understanding, highlighting how leadership infused with compassion and empathy can inspire change and promote intergenerational mobility within marginalized communities.

Other examples of leaders who embody The Protector Leadership Type include **Maria Y. Orosa**, a Filipino food scientist and war hero who developed lifesaving food technology during WWII; **Dr. Susan La Flesche Picotte**, the first Native American woman to receive a medical degree in the United States, who dedicated her life to serving and protecting the health of her Omaha tribe and bridging cultural gaps in medical care; **Ellen Johnson Sirleaf**, former Liberian president, Africa's first elected female head of state, and leading promoter of peace, justice, and democratic rule; **Elizabeth Nyamayaro**, award-winning humanitarian and former United Nations senior advisor on gender equality; **Chris Mosier**, an accomplished athlete and coach, the first transgender athlete to qualify for and compete in the Olympic trials in the gender with which they identify, and tireless advocate for transgender inclusion in sports and the rights of transgender individuals throughout society; and **Mary Mahoney**, the first licensed Black nurse in the United States, who not only broke racial barriers in the nursing profession but also dedicated her life to improving the health and well-being of the African American community, exemplifying the protective and nurturing role of a leader committed to healthcare equity and community support.

CHAMPION

Champions are inclusive leaders. They prioritize the comprehension of all perspectives of others in decision-making, and they make people feel valued. As a result, they have high levels of engagement and morale.

Motivation
Understanding through consideration and respect

Motto
"Amplify voices"

Promise
To empower and include every individual

Fear
Exclusion

Tone of Voice
- Bolstering
- Humble
- Genuine
- Empowering
- Inclusive

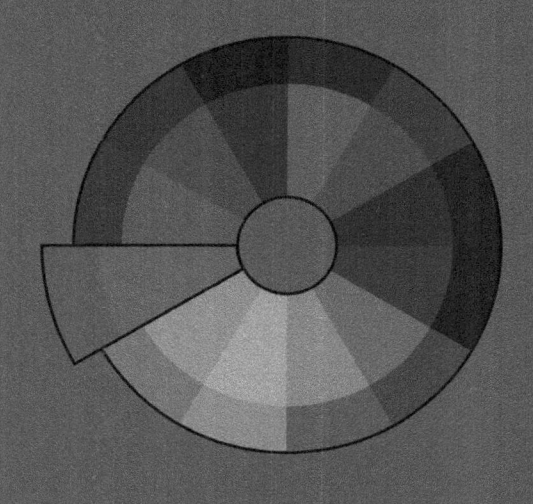

Power
To unite
- Building bridges
- Valuing diverse perspectives
- Democratizing opportunities
- Increasing representation

Influences
Simplicity and Altruism
These motivations of The Pathfinder and The Protector influence The Champion's thoughts and actions.

Amplifier
Expression
Combined with this internal motivation of The Innovator, Champions can expand their thinking and find opportunities for growth.

MEET THE CHAMPION

I fundamentally believe that when you take others' point of view and approach them in a nonjudgmental way—and vice versa—you're making the world better.

~Priscila Penha, senior design director at Google

Priscila Penha is an innovative human experience strategist with over thirty years of international expertise leading design at global technology brands, including Google, DocuSign, and Citrix Systems. Her human-centered approach to creative development prioritizes thoughtful user experiences that deliver positive outcomes.

As the senior design director at Google, Penha leads a team of designers and creators to develop inclusive digital experiences that engage Google's billions of users. She believes in the potential for virtual platforms to create change through relevant and beneficial opportunities. Her exceptional contributions to advancing Google's advertising and privacy platforms have earned her recognition as one of Google's 25 Power Players by *Business Insider*. Penha has developed cutting-edge systems that measure advertising performance across multiple platforms while protecting user privacy. She has also fostered a more collaborative environment for these initiatives, establishing Google as a leader in privacy innovation.

As an industry thought leader, Penha is passionate about reimagining digital advertising platforms to impact consumers, small businesses, and society for the better. She envisions a future in which advertising goes beyond targeting to increase access and opportunity for underserved businesses and individuals. Ultimately, Penha believes that the advertising of tomorrow can be leveraged to create a more equitable and inclusive economy by promoting products and services that benefit a wider range of people, including those who traditional marketing strategies may have previously overlooked.

With her record of innovation, as demonstrated by her contribution to new patents, Penha embodies the potential of holistic leadership to drive society forward. The patents, "Providing Enhanced Message Management User Interfaces" and "Providing Enhanced Application Interoperability," enable digital multitasking and enhance communication between digital applications. By showcasing the value of inclusive leadership in technological advancements, Penha sets an example for how diverse perspectives can lead to transformative progress in various fields.

Before joining Google, Penha served as the senior design director at DocuSign and the design director of mobile applications at Citrix. She also built an impressive portfolio as an independent designer and art director in both the UK and the United States. As a proud bilingual Latina, she champions inclusive leadership that empowers others to contribute and grow, and she is an active member of Google's Latin Leadership Counsel, Latin ERG community, and UX Leadership Council.

With her expertise in synthesizing priorities into beautiful experiences, Penha is making progress in advancing equity by both ensuring that all communities are valued and positively influencing the technologies society relies on most.

Inspired by Penha's story, let's dive deeper into her Leadership Type: The Champion.

Brief Description of The Champion

Champions are inclusive leaders. They prioritize the comprehension of all perspectives of others in decision-making, and they make people feel valued. As a result, they have high levels of engagement and morale.

Internal Motivation of The Champion

The Champion's strongest internal motivation is understanding through consideration and respect, a foundation they use to build and strengthen connections with others. The Champion's words, decisions, and actions can also be influenced by simplicity and altruism, the internal motivations of their adjacent Leadership Types (The Pathfinder and The Protector).

The greatest fear of The Champion is exclusion, which in a leadership context refers to the deliberate or unintentional act of leaving someone out, disregarding their contributions, or denying them opportunities. Exclusion contradicts The Champion's desire to actively promote inclusivity and belonging to create environments where everyone can thrive and contribute.

An energizing force or amplifier for The Champion is expression, the internal motivation of their opposite Type on the SLE, The Innovator. For The Champion, this opposing motivation can expand their thinking and be an opportunity for growth because their fight for justice can find inspiration in The Innovator's fresh perspectives. The Innovator's groundbreaking ideas can also challenge The Champion, ensuring their advocacy is both contemporary and equitable.

Greatest External Power of The Champion

The Champion's greatest external power is to unite by building bridges and valuing diverse perspectives. They can be a force to democratize opportunities and increase representation.

How The Champion Best Communicates & Relates

The Champion is an inclusive leader who establishes environments in which all contributions are valued, diverse backgrounds and skills are considered, and individual achievements are celebrated as part of the team's shared success. The Champion encourages understanding and appreciation.

To best communicate with others, here is what The Champion does:

- ✔ Values and seeks diverse input to promote inclusivity
- ✔ Respects varied perspectives in all interactions
- ✔ Encourages broad participation in forums for sharing viewpoints

✔ Involves everyone in decision-making processes

To best relate to others, here is what The Champion does:

✔ Respects the contributions of others
✔ Ensures all perspectives are heard
✔ Recognizes and appreciates the efforts of others
✔ Is an intentional listener

Key Leadership Behaviors of The Champion

The Champion is an advocate whose leadership is grounded in inclusivity and respect for others. They lead with integrity, always aligning actions and words with values, they demonstrate genuine concern for team members' perspectives and needs, and they serve as vocal advocates for equal opportunities.

When it comes to solving problems, The Champion tackles them with an inclusive mindset, ensuring all angles are considered. They engage their team in collaborative problem-solving sessions, utilizing the diverse strengths of team members for holistic solutions and prioritizing solutions that serve the broader good. To overcome obstacles, The Champion maintains high morale and elicits feedback from others. They build upon the diverse strengths of others to inform solutions and can identify lessons learned from setbacks.

To inform their decision-making, The Champion centers on understanding and fairness, promoting consensus while valuing each stakeholder's perspective. They are focused on ensuring a comprehensive understanding of the impact of a decision.

In tandem with this advocacy mindset, The Champion shapes spaces by encouraging respect and shared responsibility, stressing the value of different perspectives, and reinforcing common values within a team. When they encounter bias and barriers, they overcome them by actively challenging stereotypes within the team and organization. They implement training and awareness programs to address unconscious bias, creating pathways for underrepresented voices to be heard and recognized, and they ensure fairness in opportunities and advancements within the organization.

These combined traits allow The Champion to excel in roles that require empathy and the ability to bring people together, and they thrive when they are leading teams that benefit from a culture of understanding and mutual respect. They are at their best when they are contributing to environments that thrive on diversity and inclusive practices.

Why the World Needs More Champions

- To ensure that no voice is left unheard and no potential untapped
- To lead with a focus on equitable treatment and respect for all
- To create a more just and representative society through inclusive leadership
- To foster a sense of belonging and appreciation for every individual's contribution

Calls to Action If You Are a Champion

As The Champion Leadership Type, you can create environments where trust, empathy, and collaboration thrive. These environments maximize the team's impact and support The Champion in their quest for justice, harmony, and genuine connection. Here are some specific calls to action and ways you can realize your full leadership potential as a Champion:

→ Organize Collaborative Think Tanks
As a Champion leader, channel your motivation to build and strengthen connections by organizing regular think tank sessions. These sessions can serve as platforms for team members to share their personal and professional challenges and discuss potential solutions. By doing this,

you not only identify common interests and values but also create a supportive environment in which everyone feels valued. Here is how to execute them:
- Schedule monthly or quarterly think tank sessions.
- Encourage team members to bring up topics, challenges, or ideas they are passionate about.
- Facilitate open discussions, ensuring every voice is heard and every perspective is considered.
- Document shared values and common interests and use them as guiding principles in team decision-making processes.

→ Empower through Active Listening Workshops

One of the cornerstones of treating others with openness and honesty is the art of active listening. As a Champion leader, fostering a culture in which everyone listens empathetically can amplify the sense of trust and understanding within the team. Here is how to execute them:
- Arrange workshops or training sessions focusing on active listening skills.
- Engage in role-playing exercises where team members can practice listening without interrupting, offering solutions, or passing judgments.
- Encourage team members to provide feedback on the listening skills of their peers. This can be done anonymously if preferred.
- Make active listening a key performance indicator for team members, ensuring that it is consistently practiced and valued.

→ Share Insights and Stories

By sharing their learnings and experiences authentically and with purpose, The Champion can inspire, connect, and empower others to strive for their own success and growth. Here are some ways to get started sharing insights:
  o Write an article for LinkedIn or for submission to an industry publication that discusses the lessons you have gained from your experiences, offering ac-

tionable insights that others can apply to their own lives or work.
- Practice sharing personal stories and anecdotes to inspire others, showing them that success is possible despite challenges. Sharing struggles and triumphs can motivate others to pursue their goals with determination.
- Reach out to podcast hosts relevant to your industry and offer to share your story and lessons learned to inspire and uplift a wider audience.

Champions You Should Know

As the CEO of the Dallas Mavericks, **Cynthia Marshall** stands out as a quintessential Champion by embodying leadership that prioritizes understanding, consideration, and respect in every action and decision. Marshall's transformative influence on the Mavericks' organizational culture pivoted around her unwavering commitment to diversity, equity, and inclusion, setting a new standard for what it means to be a leader in the modern workplace. Under her guidance, the Mavericks underwent a radical cultural overhaul, introducing policies and practices that both promoted and celebrated diversity within the organization. Her approach to leadership—marked by empathy, active listening, and a genuine concern for her team's well-being—has not only improved the morale and engagement of the Mavericks' staff but has also served as a powerful model for other organizations striving for change. Marshall's ability to value and amplify diverse perspectives, creating an environment where everyone feels seen, heard, and valued, embodies the very essence of a Champion leader.

Beyond the confines of corporate leadership, Marshall's impact resonates through her community engagement and advocacy work, further illustrating her role as a Champion. She leverages her platform to advocate for social justice, education, and equality, extending her influence beyond business into the wider community. Marshall's leadership journey is a compelling narrative of overcoming personal and professional challenges, demonstrating her resilience, courage, and deep-rooted belief in the power of change. By championing the causes of diversity and inclusion, she both transforms organizations and contributes to the broader societal shift toward greater equality and understanding. Her dedication to fostering an inclusive culture where every individual can thrive showcases the transformative power of Champion leadership—a leadership style that is about not only achieving organizational goals but also empowering individuals and communities.

Another emblematic example of The Champion Leadership Type is **Dawn Staley**, an American basketball player and coach. Her journey in sports, marked by remarkable achievements both as a player and as a coach, aligns closely with the qualities that define a Champion leader. Staley's career is a testament to her ability to unite diverse groups and empower individuals, echoing the core trait of Champions who prioritize inclusivity and empathy. As a coach, she has consistently demonstrated her knack for understanding and respecting each player's unique perspective and skills, which has been instrumental in building high-performing and cohesive teams.

Moreover, Staley's internal motivation—a deep understanding and respect for others—mirrors that of a Champion. Her actions and decisions, whether as a player leading her team to victory or as a coach mentoring young athletes, have always reflected a commitment to fairness and justice. This is evident in her advocacy for gender equity in sports and her efforts to provide opportunities for underrepresented groups. As a leader, Staley embodies The Champion's characteristic approach to problem-solving: considering all angles and utilizing the strengths of team members for holistic solutions. Her ability to overcome biases and barriers, a key aspect of The Champion Leadership Type, has not only enhanced her teams' performances but also fostered an environment of mutual respect and understanding, essential characteristics for nurturing future leaders in sports and beyond.

Other examples of leaders who embody The Champion Leadership Type include **Charlotta Bass,** the first Black woman to be nominated for vice president on a national ticket by the Progressive Party and a racial and gender inclusivity advocate; **Rosario Perez**, CEO of Pro Mujer, for her commitment to empowering economically disadvantaged women in Latin America; **Justice Sandra Day O'Connor**, the first woman on the US Supreme Court, known for her unique ability to balance a divided court and her commitment to understanding different perspectives; **Mary Barra**, CEO of General Motors and leading proponent of investment in electric vehicles; **Patsy Mink**, the first woman of color elected to the US House of Representatives, the first Asian American woman to serve in Congress, and coauthor and advocate for the passage of the Title IX Amendment of the Higher Education Act, which prohibits gender discrimination by federally funded institutions of higher education; and **Dr. Alfredo Quiñones-Hinojosa**, a renowned neurosurgeon and researcher who has made significant strides in the field of brain cancer research and advocates tirelessly for equitable healthcare access, ensuring that communities around the globe have the knowledge and resources to combat this devastating disease.

CHAMPION

QUADRANT 4:
THE POWER TO STRUCTURE

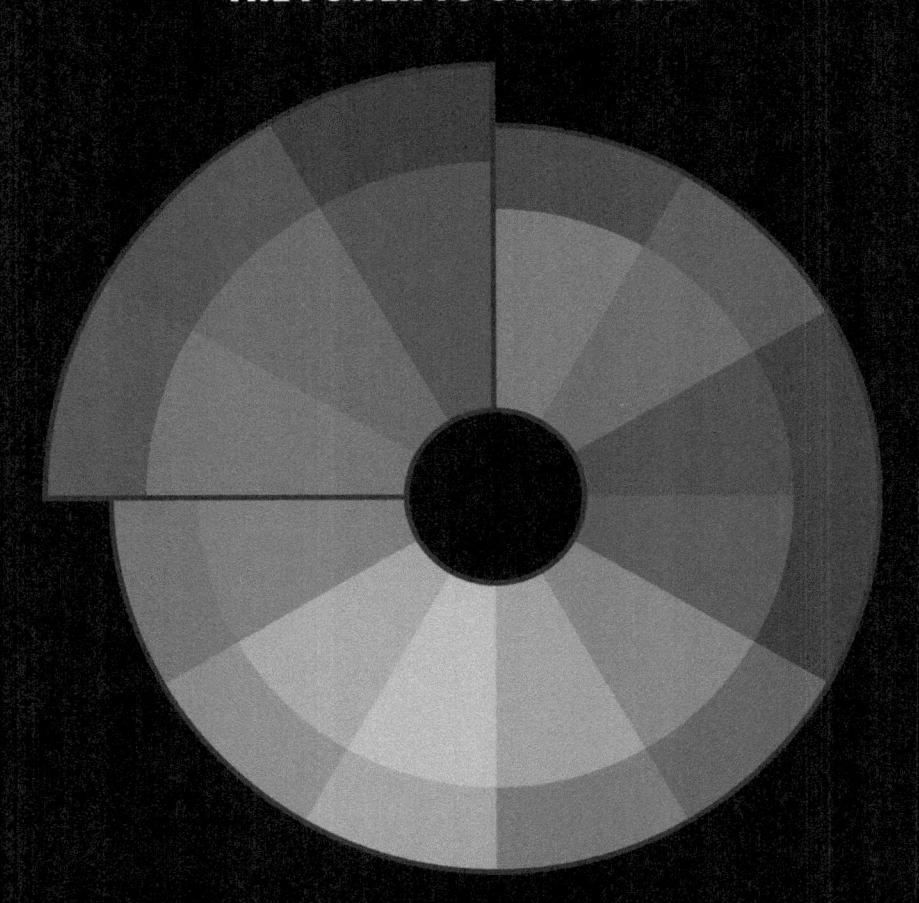

Leaders in quadrant 4 of the SLE have the power to drive systematic clarity and structured progression. They are the ones who find solace in organization, value efficiency, and aim to streamline chaos into order.

Amid such chaos and complexity, there are those who stand out with an inherent desire to bring a method to the madness. These leaders thrive on establishing order, creating roadmaps where there were once only trails, and guiding those around them toward clarity and purpose. Their drive does not stop at organizing their immediate environment; they seek to influence larger systems, ensuring they run with precision and coherence.

The Pathfinder envisions a harmonious world and aims to lay pathways that lead to it. Their focus is on channeling positive energies and using them as foundational pillars for building structured outcomes.

The Navigator, on the other hand, commands control. They see the larger picture and know the importance of influencing key elements to ensure the entire system runs smoothly. With a keen sense of command, they aim to be the driving force behind organized success.

Then there is The Guide, the harbinger of wisdom. With a deep understanding of the world, they share their insights, helping others easily navigate complexities. Their knowledge serves as a compass that directs efforts toward methodical and strategic endeavors.

Together, these leaders embody the essence of order, showcasing the immense power that comes from well-directed, organized pursuits.

PATHFINDER

Pathfinders are clarifying. They focus on what is essential in order to reduce complexities, streamline solutions, and improve operations. Their straightforward approach ensures effective and efficient outcomes.

Motivation
Simplicity through focusing on what is essential

Motto
"Light the way"

Promise
To simplify and clarify the way forward

Fear
Confusion

Tone of Voice
- Efficient
- Transparent
- Clarifying
- Straightforward
- Accessible

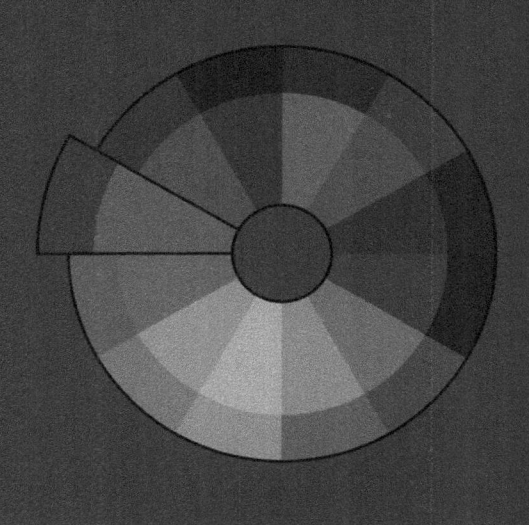

Power
To structure
- Generating clear plans
- Identifying achievable steps
- Establishing digestible methods
- Ensuring things are easy to learn

Influences
Stability and Understanding
These motivations of The Navigator and The Champion influence The Pathfinder's thoughts and actions.

Amplifier
Possibility
Combined with this internal motivation of The Trailblazer, Pathfinders can expand their thinking and find opportunities for growth.

MEET THE PATHFINDER

Impermanence puts importance on leading a life with intention.

~Kit DesLauriers, two-time World Freeskiing Women's Champion and *National Geographic*'s 2019 Adventurer of the Year

World-renowned ski mountaineer and environmental activist **Kit DesLauriers** is literally and figuratively a Pathfinder. DesLauriers's impact is wide-ranging, from being a mother, a highly accomplished athlete, and an advocate for the Arctic Refuge to being a stonemason and a sought-after storyteller, among other things. But her focus has always remained singular and constant: to lead a life of intention.

When DesLauriers skied down Mt. Everest in 2006, she became the first person in the world to climb and ski from the top of the Seven Summits, the highest mountain on each of the seven continents. Beyond the Seven Summits, DesLauriers has climbed and skied first descents in Alaska's Brooks Range, including its highest peak, and is also the first female to solo climb and ski the Grand Teton and Gannett Peak (the latter being Wyoming's highest). She also holds the honor of being the first female to descend Mt. Aspiring in New Zealand.

DesLauriers was elected to the US Ski and Snowboard Hall of Fame's Class in 2019 in recognition of her Seven Summits feat, back-to-back World Freeskiing Championships, and positive impact on the sport and society. A 20+ year member of The North Face Global Athlete Team, DesLauriers remains at the forefront of ski mountaineering. In 2015, she was named one of *National Geographic*'s Adventurers of the Year for merging science and ski mountaineering on a 2014 mapping expedition to the Arctic National Wildlife Refuge.

While her ski mountaineering resume is extensive, DesLauriers did not grow up on skis. In her memoir *Higher Love: Skiing the Seven Summits*, she writes about intentionality and how it has impacted her life's choices, including raising a wolf, moving to the mountains immediately following her graduation from the

University of Arizona, and choosing to focus on gaining the skills she needed to ski anywhere in the world.

In addition to raising two daughters in the valley of Jackson, Wyoming, (as a family they were featured in Warren Miller's 2019 film *Timeless*), DesLauriers volunteers her time and energy to protecting the Arctic National Wildlife Refuge. She has served on the American Alpine Club Board of Directors, is a long-time member of the Protect Our Winters Riders Alliance, and is currently the Board Chair for the Alaska Wilderness League.

In her 2022 documentary film, *The North Face Presents: Beyond the Summit*, DesLauriers shares her twelve-year journey, including multiple ski expeditions, to better understand and work to protect the Arctic National Wildlife Refuge from oil and gas development. Her story has the added elements of DesLauriers becoming the first person to ski the highest mountains in the US Arctic and being a critical partner in discovering which of those peaks is even the highest—another example of her showing us yet another path to see new possibilities.

Inspired by DesLauriers's intentionality and her ability to shine a spotlight on and navigate complexities, let's dive deeper into her Leadership Type: The Pathfinder.

Brief Description of The Pathfinder

Pathfinders are clarifying. They focus on what is essential in order to reduce complexities, streamline solutions, and improve operations. Their straightforward approach ensures effective and efficient outcomes.

Internal Motivation of The Pathfinder

The Pathfinder's strongest internal motivation is simplicity, or keeping a focus on what is essential. To expound on this any further would be "off-brand" for The Pathfinder. The Pathfinder's words, decisions, and actions can also be influenced by stability and understanding, the internal motivations of their adjacent Leadership Types (The Navigator and The Champion).

The greatest fear of The Pathfinder is confusion, which in a leadership context refers to a lack of clarity among team members as it relates to goals, expectations, processes, or roles. The Pathfinder knows that confusion impairs their decision-making abilities, undermines their confidence, and can negatively impact their productivity and morale.

An energizing force or amplifier for The Pathfinder is possibility, the internal motivation of their opposite Type on the SLE, The Trailblazer. For The Pathfinder, this opposing motivation can expand their thinking and be an opportunity for growth because their structured visions can find a dynamic balance in The Trailblazer's pioneering paths. The Trailblazer can introduce The Pathfinder to uncharted territories, adding excitement to their more methodical approach.

Greatest External Power of The Pathfinder

The Pathfinder's greatest external power is to structure by generating clear plans, identifying achievable steps, and establishing digestible methods. On the path to providing structure, The Pathfinder ensures that things are easy to learn for others.

How The Pathfinder Best Communicates & Relates

The Pathfinder is a pragmatic leader, known for being straightforward, setting clear expectations, and focusing on results. They encourage an action-driven environment and value efficiency and clarity.

To best communicate with others, here is what The Pathfinder does:

- ✔ Uses clear and concise language
- ✔ Avoids jargon
- ✔ Prioritizes essential information
- ✔ Streamlines communication channels for efficiency

To best relate to others, here is what The Pathfinder does:

- ✔ Is direct and honest in interactions
- ✔ Values transparency and openness
- ✔ Creates easy-to-understand and effective processes for collaboration
- ✔ Rewards clarity and practical solutions in team interactions

Key Leadership Behaviors of The Pathfinder

The Pathfinder is all about simplicity and transparency in execution. They set clear directives and expectations and consistently demonstrate the effectiveness of a straightforward, focused approach. They cut through complexity and encourage others to do the same.

When it comes to solving problems, The Pathfinder pragmatically breaks them down into their most basic elements and identifies unambiguous solutions that are easy to execute. They successfully eliminate unnecessary steps to improve problem-solving efficiency and show others a clear pathway to tackle challenges. To overcome obstacles, The Pathfinder focuses on what can be controlled and letting go of what cannot. They maintain a sense of order through organization and preparedness, creating contingency plans for various scenarios.

To inform their decision-making, The Pathfinder weighs options based on simplicity and effectiveness. They cut through ambiguity to reach the core of issues, value straightforward solutions, and prioritize actions that offer clear and measurable benefits.

In tandem with this straightforward thinking, The Pathfinder shapes spaces by promoting efficiency and simplicity. They encourage alignment by discouraging overcomplication and celebrating practicality. When they encounter bias and barriers, they overcome them by cutting through complexity that may hide systemic biases and streamlining processes to reduce barriers to entry or progress. They address preconceptions by focusing on essential facts and encourage merit-based recognition that values practical results.

These combined traits allow The Pathfinder to excel in roles that require organizational efficiency, and they thrive in environments where clear direction is valued. They can be a force for simplification, particularly when complexity reduction in systems or procedures is required.

Why the World Needs More Pathfinders

- To provide clarity in a world overwhelmed by complexity
- To streamline processes for better productivity and understanding
- To lead by example to demonstrate the power of a focused approach
- To help others focus on what is most essential

Calls to Action If You Are a Pathfinder

As The Pathfinder Leadership Type, you have the ability to cast a spotlight on what matters most to best guide those around you. Your optimism about the future is balanced with your ability to set pragmatic strategies with actionable steps. By focusing on results and resources, you can transform your aspirations into measurable impact for your team and the wider community. Here are some specific calls to action and ways you can realize your full leadership potential as a Pathfinder:

→ Champion and Realize Your Vision
While your optimistic viewpoint is a strength, others may not always mirror it. As a leader, ensuring that you have the requisite support, tools, and strategies to materialize your aspirations is pivotal. Here are the steps to take:
- Arrange structured brainstorming sessions, creating a conducive environment where ideas can be freely shared and refined collaboratively.

- Seek out mentors or peers who mirror your leadership style for insights, ensuring continuous growth and learning.
- Prioritize training modules that sharpen your communication skills, enabling you to convey your vision compellingly and effectively.

→ Lead with Proactive Planning

Developing a strategic plan is critical to setting clear direction, aligning resources, managing risks, and promoting accountability and transparency within a team or organization. Here are the steps to take:
- Volunteer to design or draft the annual plan for your team or department.
- Use your understanding of historical trends and foresight into the upcoming year to guide your strategy.

→ Seek Out New Perspectives

Engaging with a wider range of stakeholders, including customers, clients, suppliers, and industry experts (within and outside of your industry), can provide new and valuable insights to help inform your decision-making. Here are the steps to take:
- Subscribe to industry publications, newsletters, and blogs to follow thought leaders and influencers on social media and expand your own thinking.
- Attend conferences, webinars, or networking events to stay up to speed with developments in your field.
- Actively seek out and participate in innovative forums and conventions beyond your industry.

Pathfinders You Should Know

Through her revolutionary KonMari Method, **Marie Kondo** embodies the quintessence of a Pathfinder leader through her dedication to simplifying the complexities of clutter, not just in physical spaces but in life itself. Her philosophy transcends the act of tidying up to offer a straightforward, structured approach to identifying what truly brings joy and value to a person's life. Kondo's method is a masterclass in clarifying and streamlining, and it is teaching millions worldwide to focus on the essential and discard the superfluous. This act of focusing on what is truly important is what makes Kondo a Pathfinder—she lights the way for others to follow a path of simplicity, leading to more organized, fulfilled lives. Her approach is not just about physical decluttering but about setting clear, achievable steps toward a more intentional and meaningful existence. She embodies The Pathfinder's power to generate clear plans and establish digestible methods for complex challenges.

Moreover, Kondo's impact as a Pathfinder is evident in the fact that her method has infiltrated various aspects of culture and industry, from home organization to workplace efficiency and mental health. By encouraging a focus on joy and simplicity, Kondo has clarified the path toward not just a tidier closet but a more harmonious life. Her tone, both in her books and television appearances, is consistently efficient, transparent, and accessible, making the process of decluttering and organizing not a daunting task but an achievable, even enjoyable, journey. Kondo's ability to make her method easy to learn and adopt worldwide demonstrates her innate capacity as a Pathfinder to simplify and clarify, ensuring that her straightforward approach to tidying up is a sustainable, life-changing philosophy. Through her work, Kondo offers a clear promise to simplify and clarify the way forward, guiding millions to discover the joy of simplicity, both in their surroundings and in their lives.

Another emblematic example of The Pathfinder Leadership Type is **Xiuhtezcatl Martinez**, a young environmental activist who has been at the forefront of the youth-led environmental movement, advocating for strong action on climate change and working toward a sustainable future. His efforts to simplify the global conversation around environmental issues and to make activism accessible and actionable for young people worldwide demonstrate his ability to light the way toward environmental sustainability and justice.

Martinez's approach to environmental activism is characterized by generating clear, achievable plans and establishing digestible methods for engagement, making the fight against climate change more approachable for individuals and communities. His work in mobilizing youth and influencing policy decisions highlights his talent for clarifying complex problems and leading the charge toward effective solutions. By focusing on essential actions and empowering others with the knowledge and tools to make a difference, Martinez exemplifies The Pathfinder's commitment to simplifying and clarifying the path forward in the pursuit of environmental justice and sustainability.

Other examples of leaders who embody The Pathfinder Leadership Type include **Dr. Patricia E. Bath**, an ophthalmologist and inventor whose invention of the laserphaco probe for cataract surgery demonstrates her innovative spirit and commitment to improving medical procedures; **Doris Lessing**, a writer whose work tackled complex subjects such as race relations and human sexuality with simplicity, directness, and understandable narratives; **Rachel Carson**, an inspiring pioneer in the world of environmental science and conservation whose book *Silent Spring* alerted the public to the dangers of using chemical pesticides; **Daymond John**, founder, president, and CEO of FUBU, who appears as an investor on the ABC reality television series *Shark Tank*; **Ellen Ochoa**, a pioneering astronaut and the first Latina to go to space, who later served as the director of the Johnson Space Center, leading and inspiring countless individuals to explore STEM fields and space exploration with her visionary outlook and commitment to education and innovation; and **Indra Nooyi**, former CEO of PepsiCo, who redefined the global food and beverage industry with a focus on healthy products and sustainability, leading her company through significant transformation with her clear, forward-thinking strategies.

NAVIGATOR

Navigators are stabilizers. They are steady under pressure and foster a sense of security and confidence in others. Their approach is systematic and process-oriented, making them dependable and reliable leaders.

Motivation
Stability to ensure order

Motto
"Drive success"

Promise
To steer with strategy and focus

Fear
Chaos

Tone of Voice
- Focused
- Motivating
- Stable
- Refined
- Strategic

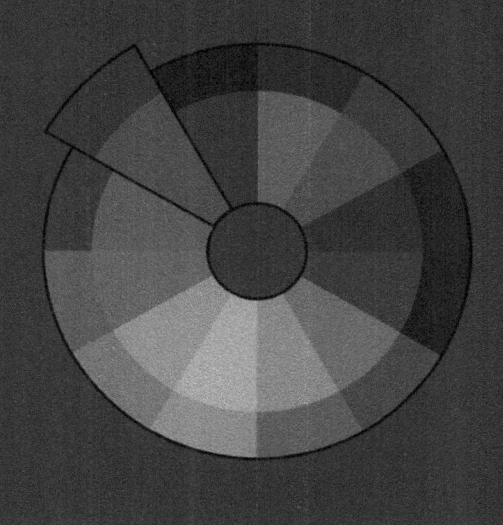

Power
To structure
- Driving strategies
- Enhancing productivity
- Advancing operational capabilities
- Systematically approaching problem-solving

Influences
Simplicity and Knowledge
These motivations of The Pathfinder and The Guide influence The Navigator's thoughts and actions.

Amplifier
Liberation
Combined with this internal motivation of The Catalyst, Navigators can expand their thinking and find opportunities for growth.

MEET THE NAVIGATOR

I bring a lot of structure to others, but my intent is not to be too rigid. It's about assessing the current landscape, bringing the structure in, and optimizing the way that people do things, challenging them to look at their work in a different way.

~Teddra Burgess, managing director of civilian sales at Google Public Sector

Teddra Burgess, a seasoned tech executive, public sector solutions strategist, and equitable access advocate, has been instrumental in driving digital transformation for government and commercial entities around the world. With over twenty-five years of experience leading sales, engineering, business development, strategic partnerships, marketing, and operations, she is committed to bettering the citizen experience through technology, access, inclusive leadership, and people empowerment.

Burgess's impact in the public sector spans over two decades, during which she has fostered strategic partnerships and driven success as an award-winning tech executive. Over the course of her career, she has showcased her commitment to improving the "citizen experience." Most recently she has focused on leveraging technology to help federal agencies meet the call for improved access, experience, and cybersecurity, outlined in Executive Orders such as the Executive Order on Transforming Federal Customer Experience and Service Delivery to Rebuild Trust in Government and the Executive Order on Improving the Nation's Cybersecurity. She describes the Federal Civilian agencies as being an industry of industries, supporting a myriad of missions from education, to science, to health, to transportation, and many more. She relishes the opportunity to make a positive impact on society driving inclusivity, public service access, and opportunity for all.

Burgess's previous roles include senior vice president of Public Sector at Tanium, vice president at ASG Technologies, Chief

Revenue Officer at Micro Focus Government Solutions, and various leadership roles at both Micro Focus and Hewlett Packard Enterprise. Her leadership is underscored by numerous accolades, including being a four-time CRN Women of the Channel honoree, winning over twenty quarterly and annual corporate sales awards, and receiving industry recognition for her leadership by FedScoop, WashExec, and Chief.

Currently, as the managing director of civilian sales at Google Public Sector, Burgess is at the forefront of providing leading cloud and artificial intelligence technologies to federal civilian agencies in order to drive efficiency and effectiveness. An advocate for women+ and people of color in technology, Burgess is an independent angel investor with Pipeline Angels, BLXVC, and a founding member of the women's network Chief in Washington, DC. Fueled by the belief that inclusive leadership drives more access, her thought leadership on the Google Summit stage has focused on ways to expand that access through artificial intelligence and machine learning. Her contributions to outlets such as Bloomberg and the Institute for Critical Infrastructure Technology (ICIT) ensure a focus remains on cybersecurity and other citizen protections.

Inspired by Burgess's story, let's dive deeper into her Leadership Type: The Navigator.

Brief Description of The Navigator

Navigators are stabilizers. They are steady under pressure and foster a sense of security and confidence in others. Their approach is systematic and process-oriented, making them dependable and reliable leaders.

Internal Motivation of The Navigator

The Navigator's strongest internal motivation is stability, or to ensure order. They seek to lead and gain control in order to best provide for those around them. The Navigator's words, decisions, and actions can also be influenced by knowledge and simplicity, the internal motivations of their adjacent Leadership Types (The Pathfinder and The Guide).

The greatest fear of The Navigator is chaos, which in a leadership context refers to the state of disorder or unpredictability within an organization. Chaos diminishes The Navigator's abilities to maintain focus and control and provide direction.

An energizing force or amplifier for The Navigator is liberation, the internal motivation of their opposite Type on the SLE, The Catalyst. For The Navigator, this opposing motivation can expand their thinking and be an opportunity for growth because their relentless momentum can be energized by The Catalyst's awakening energy. The Catalyst can breathe life into The Navigator's actions, making every move both swift and meaningful.

Greatest External Power of The Navigator

The Navigator's greatest external power is to structure by driving strategies and systematically approaching problem-solving. On the path to providing structure, The Navigator advances operational capabilities and enhances productivity.

How The Navigator Best Communicates & Relates

The Navigator is a structured and progress-oriented leader, known for promoting reliability and expertise, establishing clear roles and responsibilities, and creating systematic processes. They value consistency and quality.

To best communicate with others, here is what The Navigator does:

- ✔ Employs structured communication
- ✔ Provides consistent updates and feedback
- ✔ Focuses on moving things forward
- ✔ Encourages methodical approaches to problem-solving

To best relate to others, here is what The Navigator does:

- ✓ Builds trust through dependability and consistency
- ✓ Prioritizes one-on-one interactions to understand individual needs
- ✓ Fosters professional growth through stable support
- ✓ Keeps open lines of communication for reliability

Key Leadership Behaviors of The Navigator

The Navigator excels in creating a stable and dependable environment, focusing on structured processes and systematic approaches. They lead by example by establishing a consistent framework within which team members can operate. This stability is key to fostering confidence and reliability, making The Navigator an anchor in tumultuous times. They prioritize clear, structured communication and provide regular updates and feedback, ensuring that everyone is aligned and moving forward together.

When it comes to solving problems, The Navigator approaches them with a methodical and logical mindset, relying on established routines and processes. They analyze challenges logically by breaking them down into manageable components and employing best practices and proven methodologies to find practical solutions. By keeping a long-term perspective, The Navigator maneuvers short-term obstacles with ease, maintaining a sense of calm and assurance that permeates their team.

To inform their decision-making, The Navigator analyzes the potential for long-term stability, weighing the benefits of structure versus flexibility. They consider the impact of a decision on systems and processes, aiming for sustainable and pragmatic solutions.

In tandem with a logical mindset, The Navigator minimizes bias and promotes a culture of objective decision-making by implementing fair and standardized procedures. They build systems that support equitable opportunities for all, addressing barriers through careful optimization of processes. This structured approach ensures that decisions are made based on merit and practical results, reinforcing The Navigator's commitment to fairness and efficiency. Navigators are strategic planners and are adept at enhancing operational capabilities and driving strategies that advance the organization's goals.

These combined traits allow The Navigator to excel in roles that demand a high degree of organization and precision, leading sectors where dependability and strategic planning are critical. By streamlining processes and applying a strategic focus, they improve problem-solving efficiency and prioritize long-term stability, ensuring that the organization remains focused and effective.

Why the World Needs More Navigators

- To provide a calming presence in the face of uncertainty
- To ensure a stable foundation for growth and development
- To maintain order and enhance productivity in all operations
- To offer reliable leadership that instills confidence

Calls to Action If You Are a Navigator

As The Navigator Leadership Type, you work to ensure that others understand and can lean into the structure and processes you provide, so ensuring that you remain open to new possibilities and the unique contributions of others is key to expanding your impact. Here are some specific calls to action and ways you can realize your full leadership potential as a Navigator:

→ Lead Structured, Yet Flexible Strategic Planning Sessions
Strategic planning is a structured approach you can take to define your team's or organization's long-term goals

and objectives, determine the actions needed to achieve those goals, and allocate resources accordingly. Here are the steps to take:
- Ensure that all key stakeholders are involved in the strategic planning sessions.
- Encourage participation from diverse perspectives to foster creativity and innovation.
- Employ a range of facilitation techniques to encourage participation and engagement.
- Remain flexible and adaptable throughout the sessions to accommodate unexpected changes or developments.

→ Disrupt Yourself

Consider trying new things outside your comfort zone to gain a new perspective and add to your storytelling as a leader. Here are the steps to take:
- Try a new hobby that challenges your ability to navigate effectively.
- Move your skill set to a completely new industry to take on the next challenge.
- Prioritize not getting stuck in one position too long because of the ease of the work.

→ Promote Problem-Solving and Operational Excellence

Emphasize a systematic approach to problem-solving to enhance team effectiveness. Here are the steps to take:
- Implement process improvement workshops to identify and eliminate pitfalls in workflows.
- Encourage team members to approach challenges with a logical and pragmatic mindset, focusing on practical solutions.
- Share best practices and proven methodologies with your team to standardize approaches to common challenges.

Navigators You Should Know

Alexandria Ocasio-Cortez is a prime example of The Navigator Leadership Type. Since her election to Congress, she has consistently demonstrated a strategic focus on key issues for sustainable societal change. Ocasio-Cortez has championed progressive policies such as the Green New Deal and Medicare for All, showcasing her clear and practical approach to complex societal challenges. Her leadership style is marked by directness, transparency, and a firm commitment to efficient and pragmatic decision-making.

A defining aspect of Ocasio-Cortez's leadership is her visionary yet structured advocacy for comprehensive climate action. The Green New Deal, a central initiative she spearheaded, aims to address climate change while creating economic opportunity. This ambitious plan mirrors The Navigator's strategy of breaking down monumental challenges into actionable and systematic steps. It not only positions her as a leader in environmental advocacy but also reflects her straightforward approach in tackling such complex issues. By focusing on practical, sustainable solutions and maintaining a long-term perspective, Ocasio-Cortez exemplifies the fundamental traits of a Navigator leader.

Another emblematic example of The Navigator Leadership Type is **Troy Polamalu**. His tenure with the Pittsburgh Steelers in the NFL was marked by strategic foresight and a systematic approach that transcended the gridiron. His exceptional football IQ allowed him to anticipate and disrupt the opposition's strategies, effectively steering his team through the tumultuous waters of high-stakes games. Polamalu's leadership was not just about personal accolades; it was about enhancing the operational capabilities of his team, making every play and every decision count toward collective success.

Beyond his legendary status on the field, Polamalu has made contributions off the field that have further cemented his reputation as a Navigator. His philanthropic initiatives that aim to provide support and resources to communities in need showcase his methodical approach to solving societal issues. By applying the same focus and strategic planning to his charitable work that he did in football, Polamalu has made significant impacts that go beyond temporary aid to drive long-term improvements and stability. His ability to remain composed under pressure, whether facing a formidable opponent on the field or tackling societal challenges, instills a sense of confidence and security in those around him, truly embodying The Navigator's promise to steer with strategy and focus.

Other examples of leaders who embody The Navigator Leadership Type include **Ayanna Pressley**, a member of the US House of Representatives, known for her systematic approach to advocacy and policy-making, particularly in areas such as criminal justice reform and women's rights; **Zhang Xin**, who rose from homelessness to become a leading real estate developer in China through a systematic approach to process optimization and strategic development; **Pramila Jayapal**, a US Representative and chair of the Congressional Progressive Caucus who is recognized for her strategic and structured approach in pushing for healthcare reform and workers' rights; **Lidiane Jones**, a product manager turned leading tech CEO known for being pragmatic, practical, and insightful; **Dr. Atul Gawande**, a renowned surgeon, writer, and public health researcher who applies a systematic and process-oriented approach to tackling complex healthcare challenges, ensuring efficient and effective patient care and safety protocols; and **Katharine Graham**, the former publisher of the *Washington Post*, whose leadership and strategic decision-making steered the newspaper through the tumultuous Watergate scandal, exemplifying her ability to navigate high-pressure situations with grace and determination.

GUIDE

Guides are lifelong learners. They believe that facts and data are ever-evolving assets that enhance people, ideas, and organizations, and they want to know how and why things work in order to inform decisions and strategies.

Motivation
Knowledge through intellectual curiosity

Motto
"Share wisdom"

Promise
To enlighten with knowledge and insight

Fear
Ignorance

Tone of Voice
- Reliable
- Objective
- Curious
- Wise
- Thoughtful

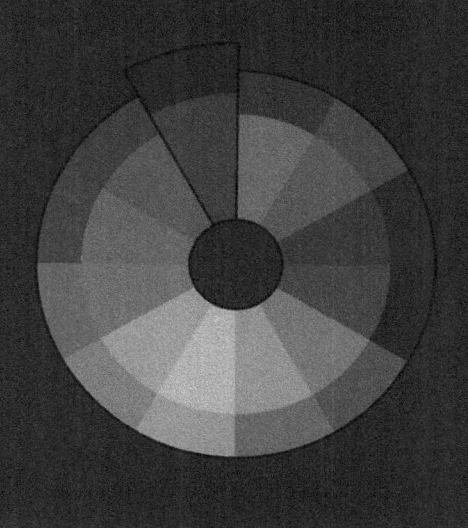

Power
To structure
- Identifying facts
- Sharing insights
- Analyzing trends
- Encouraging curiosity

Influences
Realization and Stability
These motivations of The Visionary and The Navigator influence The Guide's thoughts and actions.

Amplifier
Enjoyment
Combined with this internal motivation of The Ignitor, Guides can expand their thinking and find opportunities for growth.

MEET THE GUIDE

I believe that curiosity not only fosters our community or ancestral knowledge but also brings us joy. When we're curious about something and have the autonomy and opportunity to explore it further, it leads to a deep sense of fulfillment.

~Ashley Brailsford, founder of Unearthing Joy

During her time as a first- through third-grade teacher, early childhood professor, and family literacy program director, **Ashley Brailsford** felt joy was missing from our educational system. She realized that when it comes to our nature's history, most lessons, courses, and experiences are taught from the perspective of those who are White, while the experiences of Black, Indigenous, and other people of color—the global majority—too often go untold. She founded Unearthing Joy to uncover those stories, uplift our ancestors and their contributions, and inspire joy for all Earth's children, families, and communities.

Brailsford is committed to helping families and communities, especially those who have been historically excluded, find joy in nature as she has throughout her own life, and Unearthing Joy is determined to make that a reality. Driven by a passion for inclusive education and a deep connection with nature, Brailsford has taken a journey as an educator and leader that has been marked by her unwavering commitment to bringing joy and diversity into learning environments. Her work with Unearthing Joy reflects her personal philosophy that nature's history should be inclusive and representative of all cultures and backgrounds.

Brailsford's extensive background in early childhood education and family literacy, as well as her professorship in these fields, has greatly influenced the culturally inclusive, nature-based programming at Unearthing Joy. Her personal experiences as an outdoor guide and nature enthusiast have been instrumental in shaping the organization's unique approach to learning and exploration. Under her guidance, Unearthing Joy has not only developed a PhD-backed, nationally recognized curriculum but also created immersive experiences and workshops that honor the contributions of Black, Indigenous, and other people of color. Her leadership emphasizes the importance of recognizing our historically excluded ancestors, ensuring their stories are a central part of the learning journey.

Brailsford's vision extends beyond curriculum development to celebrating the lived experiences of community members and their knowledge, fostering spaces where families and communities can connect with nature in meaningful and joyous ways. Her dedication to this mission has made Unearthing Joy a great source of hope and inspiration, embodying the principles of diversity, inclusion, and joy in every aspect of its operations.

Inspired by Brailsford's story, let's dive deeper into her Leadership Type: The Guide.

Brief Description of The Guide

Guides are lifelong learners. They believe that facts and data are ever-evolving assets that enhance people, ideas, and organizations, and they want to know how and why things work in order to inform decisions and strategies.

Internal Motivation of The Guide

The Guide's strongest internal motivation is knowledge. They are intellectually curious and possess independence in thought and action, and they provide wisdom and mentorship while equipping others to help them navigate challenges and reach their full potential. The Guide's words, decisions, and actions can also be influenced by realization and stability, the internal motivations of their adjacent Leadership Types (The Visionary and The Navigator).

The greatest fear of The Guide is ignorance, which in a leadership context refers to a failure to acquire, interpret, or utilize knowledge effectively. Ignorance hinders The Guide's ability to gain new insights as well as their pursuit of growth.

An energizing force or amplifier for The Guide is enjoyment, the internal motivation of their opposite Type on the SLE, The Ignitor. For The Guide, this opposing motivation can expand their thinking and be an opportunity for growth because their wisdom can be illuminated by The Ignitor's positivity. The Ignitor can help illuminate The Guide's insights, harmonizing depth with more of a sense of joy and delight.

Greatest External Power of The Guide

The Guide's greatest external power is to structure by analyzing trends, identifying facts, and sharing insights. On the path to providing structure, The Guide encourages curiosity in others.

How The Guide Best Communicates & Relates

The Guide is a knowledge-driven leader who is known for their analytical approach. They promote continuous learning, knowledge sharing, and cross-functional understanding.

To best communicate with others, here is what The Guide does:

- ✔ Bases communications on facts
- ✔ Shares insights based on findings
- ✔ Offers explanations to enhance understanding
- ✔ Uses questions to encourage curiosity

To best relate to others, here is what The Guide does:

- ✔ Engages through shared interests in learning
- ✔ Builds relationships based on mutual intellectual growth
- ✔ Facilitates meaningful conversations that stimulate thought
- ✔ Respects diverse viewpoints and expertise

Key Leadership Behaviors of The Guide

The Guide leads by example in their continuous learning and development. They consistently emphasize the importance of staying informed and educated, thereby encouraging an organizational thirst for knowledge. They can be trusted and relied on to make decisions with a clear and informed rationale.

When it comes to solving problems, The Guide leverages a systematic and analytical framework, gathering and dissecting information to identify the root causes. They encourage a collaborative approach to problem-solving with informed discussions and then apply critical thinking to develop innovative solutions. To overcome obstacles, The Guide delves deep into data and facts to seek out logical solutions. They rely on research and information to navigate uncertainty, and they take the time to process and learn from challenges and setbacks.

To inform their decision-making, The Guide utilizes a data-driven approach, weighing options based on research and analysis. They consider the long-term implications of decisions through a knowledge lens and aim for strategic and informed choices.

In tandem with their thirst for knowledge, The Guide shapes spaces by focusing on facts to promote shared understanding and fostering evidence-based decision-making. They celebrate curiosity and continuous learning by recognizing and rewarding intellectual growth. When they encounter bias and barriers, they overcome them by promoting the use of data to counter subjective biases, encouraging openness to new information and perspectives. They seek to implement systems that ensure decisions are fact-based, and they create avenues for every team member to access learning and counteract ignorance.

These combined traits allow The Guide to thrive in environments that value expertise and informed decisions. They fit well into roles that require deep understanding and strategic planning and can make significant contributions to knowledge-driven industries and sectors.

Why the World Needs More Guides

- To combat misinformation and ignorance with informed insights

- To lead organizations toward more educated and strategic operations
- To ensure that decisions are based on a foundation of knowledge and facts
- To inspire a culture in which learning and expertise are valued and fostered

Calls to Action If You Are a Guide

As The Guide Leadership Type, you focus your essence as a leader on sharing wisdom and facilitating growth in others. Your journey of learning is perpetual, and you are consistently receptive to acquiring new knowledge and insights. A harmonious relationship between you and those eager to learn can help create an organizational culture characterized by respect, evolution, and advancement. Here are some specific calls to action and ways you can realize your full leadership potential as a Guide:

→ Cultivate a Culture of Learning

As a Guide, your natural inclination toward knowledge and wisdom can set the tone for your entire team or organization. Embrace this role and create an environment that prioritizes continuous learning and the exchange of insights. Here are some action steps to take:
- Initiate regular sessions where you can share your insights, experiences, and lessons with your team. These sessions can foster a culture of open dialogue and mutual growth.
- Implement an open-door policy, inviting team members to come forward with questions or to seek advice. This will position you as a trusted mentor and strengthen team cohesion.
- Whether it is books, courses, or workshops, dedicate resources for your own continuous learning. A well-rounded knowledge base will empower you to offer diverse perspectives and solutions.

→ Champion Mentorship Initiatives

Your strength as a Guide is magnified when you actively mentor others, assisting them in navigating their professional and personal challenges. Here are some action steps to take:

- Establish mentorship programs within your team or organization. By pairing newer team members with more experienced professionals, you nurture a platform for skill and knowledge transfer.
- Organize consistent check-ins between mentors and mentees. A structured approach ensures that the mentorship remains goal-oriented and beneficial.
- Embrace the concept of reverse mentoring. By being open to learning from younger team members, you ensure you stay attuned to fresh perspectives and emerging trends.

→ Consider Pursuing More Public-Facing Opportunities To Serve Others

Public-facing experiences and roles expose leaders to a wide range of perspectives, challenges, and opportunities. Engaging with a wider range of stakeholders can enrich The Guide's understanding of complex issues and foster a more nuanced approach to compromise, alignment, and sharing their insights with conviction. Here are some action steps to take:

- Become a volunteer board member for a local non-profit organization aligned with a cause or a purpose that matters to you.
- Consider running for public office. These types of positions can be great opportunities to positively influence your community, engage with diverse perspectives, and make meaningful contributions to the common good.
- Seek out committee or board roles. Serving on a board typically involves a high degree of accountability, responsibility, and transparency, making these types of roles particularly appealing to The Guide.

Guides You Should Know

The late Jokichi Takamine seamlessly embodies the archetype of The Guide through his groundbreaking scientific contributions and efforts to foster cultural understanding and appreciation. His isolation of adrenaline marked a pivotal moment in medical history, showcasing his deep commitment to advancing human knowledge and health. Beyond his scientific achievements, Takamine is dedicated to bridging cultural divides between Japan and the United States, highlighting his role as a Guide. By donating two thousand cherry trees to Washington, DC, he not only enhanced the physical landscape but also offered a lasting symbol of friendship and mutual respect between two nations. This act of generosity was rooted in his belief in the power of knowledge and cultural exchange to enlighten and unify people across diverse backgrounds.

Takamine's life and work reflect a profound commitment to sharing wisdom and encouraging curiosity. His scientific achievements provided critical insights into the human body's mechanisms, significantly enhancing medical research and treatment. Meanwhile, his philanthropic endeavors demonstrated a thoughtful approach to international relations, emphasizing the importance of understanding and appreciating different cultures. Through his actions, Takamine lived by The Guide's motto to "share wisdom," using his knowledge and resources to benefit society and promote cross-cultural understanding. His legacy is one of enlightenment, characterized by a relentless pursuit of knowledge and a deep desire to structure opportunities for learning and growth, both within his field and in the broader community.

Another emblematic example of The Guide Leadership Type is **Jane Goodall**, an ethologist and conservationist renowned for her groundbreaking work with chimpanzees. Her lifelong dedication to the study of primates and her extensive field research revolutionized our understanding of animal behavior and human primatology. Goodall's passion for conservation and her efforts to share her findings have inspired generations to pursue knowledge and care for the natural world. Her transformative journey began when she traveled to Gombe Stream National Park in Tanzania in 1960. With little more than a notebook and binoculars, she embarked on what would become a legendary study of chimpanzee behavior. Her discovery that chimpanzees make and use tools challenged the then-prevailing beliefs about the intellectual capabilities of animals and redefined the relationship between humans and the animal kingdom. Goodall's continued advocacy for environmental stewardship and her founding of the Jane Goodall Institute solidify her role as a Guide, continuously shaping our ideas about conservation and our place in the natural world.

Other examples of leaders who embody The Guide Leadership Type include **LeVar Burton**, an actor, director, and educator known for his role in *Reading Rainbow*, where he inspired a love of reading and learning in children by presenting literature and educational content in an engaging manner; **Neil deGrasse Tyson**, an astrophysicist known for his ability to make complex scientific concepts accessible and engaging to the public; **Jaime Escalante**, a highly regarded educator known for his work in teaching advanced mathematics to underprivileged students in East Los Angeles, demonstrating his deep commitment to learning and student development; **Emily Glassberg Sands**, a data scientist and economist who is fueling data-driven decisions and building data-powered solutions for leading global organizations; **Ursula Burns**, the first African American woman to serve as CEO of a Fortune 500 company, who has mentored young women and minorities in the fields of science and engineering, guiding them toward fulfilling careers; and **Isabel Mavrides-Calderón**, a dynamic Latina disability justice activist and organizer who has led significant campaigns and consultations to enhance accessibility and combat ableism, proving herself a vital Guide in the advocacy and policy landscape for disability rights.

FIND YOUR LEADERSHIP TYPE

Now that you have learned more about each of the 12 Leadership Types, you have probably begun to see yourself and others in several of them. As you attempt to narrow them down, there are a few caveats to keep in mind: 1) leaders tend to identify with a primary Leadership Type, but secondary Leadership Types are important to consider and explore; 2) a person's Leadership Type can change and evolve over time depending on context, goals, and where they are in their career life cycle; and 3) Leadership Types are intended to help guide you as a leader, but they are not a "set it and forget it" approach—they are as dynamic as you are.

Here are some self-reflection prompts intended to help you dig deeper and begin to draw some connections between the Leadership Types and your own experiences, observations, and aspirations. Your answers will provide valuable insights into your leadership journey and the path you wish to tread in the future. As you progress, keep these reflections at hand. They serve as a reminder that effective leadership is as much about understanding ourselves as it is about understanding those we lead.

→ As you explored the various Leadership Types, which one did you resonate with most closely and why? Does it align with your current leadership style, or does it represent the leader you aspire to be?

→ Identify the Leadership Type you most associate with. Think about a situation in which you embodied its characteristics. Where were you, who were you with, and what were you doing? What did it feel like?

→ Breaking free from traditional leadership molds and embracing a diverse set of Leadership Types can lead to more inclusive and innovative environments. Reflect on a time when you or someone you know went against conventional leadership norms. What were the results, and how did it impact the team or organization?

→ Understanding and embodying your Leadership Type can be a transformative journey that leads to personal growth, self-efficacy, and fulfillment. How can recognizing and embracing your Leadership Type influence your personal and professional growth journey?

→ Tailoring communication based on your Leadership Type and understanding that of others can enhance clarity, reduce conflicts, and drive alignment. Reflect on a communication challenge you faced in a leadership capacity. With your new understanding of Leadership Types, how could the situation have been approached differently for a better outcome?

→ Fill in the blanks:

→ I can identify _____ as an example of the _____ Leadership Type in my team/organization/industry. The qualities or characteristics of their leadership that I most admire are _____.

→ In situations involving _____, I would collaborate effectively with someone who embodies the _____ Leadership Type.

→ Previously, I felt more like a _____ Leadership Type, but recent experiences have made me lean more toward the _____ Leadership Type.

→ Had I known about my inclination toward the _____ Leadership Type, I would have handled the situation with _____ differently by _____.

While reading this book and practicing self-reflection are great first steps in the journey toward greater awareness and understanding of the range of Leadership Types, identifying your own Leadership Type is more nuanced. Doing so requires you to think deeply about things that are highly personal and unique to you, such as your purpose, mission, vision, values, and internal motivation. It also requires you to think deeply about your impact on others and how you best relate to and communicate with them, which is something that is difficult to do on your own. An outside perspective on your leadership coming from a trusted source can be essential, and that is where our team at BREAKTHRU can provide expert guidance.

To that end, we invite you to visit LeadershipTypes.com to take our Leadership Types quiz. In taking this free, five-minute survey, discover which Leadership Type or power quadrant is potentially most relevant to, or fitting for, you given your current or aspirational role as a leader. Learn about what specific Leadership Types may align with your leadership style, motivations, and strengths based on your responses.

Depending on where you are at in your leadership journey and your current context, your quiz results may be more or less definitive. Based on BREAKTHRU's work with clients, individuals with more definitive results (indicating a primary Leadership Type) are best equipped to lead effectively and begin to build clear, cohesive, and impactful brands as leaders. Individuals with less definitive or more scattered results in terms of their Leadership Type present a unique opportunity for a deeper assessment and may benefit from additional, expert guidance. We have seen that individuals with more scattered results are often seeking role clarity or are in moments of inflection or career transition. We have also seen that members of underrepresented groups who express the need to code-switch, or adjust the way they communicate with and relate to others in the workplace, tend to have more scattered results because they feel like they constantly need to adapt to fit into the dominant culture rather than express their individuality as leaders.

For all of you seeking to explore your Leadership Type more deeply and take it into action in more specific ways based on your unique context and goals, we invite you to consider collaborating directly with our team at BREAKTHRU to set you on a path to unlock and realize your full potential. Reach out to us via hello@breakthrubrands.com to set up a time to speak with someone on our team to better determine whether our customized leadership development approach is a fit for you, members of your team, or your entire organization.

TAKE THE LEADERSHIP TYPES INTO ACTION

By understanding their Leadership Types, leaders can be more intentional in their leadership, shaping their strategies and approaches according to their strengths and greatest powers. With the increasing demand for transparency and accountability in leadership roles, understanding and aligning with a specific Leadership Type can help leaders remain grounded because each serves as a continuous reminder of their core values and leadership ethos. When faced with ethical dilemmas or challenging decisions, a leader can reflect on their own or someone else's Leadership Type to guide them back to their fundamental principles and ensure their decisions are consistent with their intrinsic motivations, values, and beliefs. This has wide-reaching implications for individuals, teams, organizations, industries, and the world.

By identifying with a particular Leadership Type, leaders can recognize areas of strength and potential growth. For instance, if you are an Ignitor who excels at creating positive atmospheres, you can see how you might benefit from emulating some attributes of your amplifier, The Guide, to deepen your knowledge base and expertise. By recognizing the inherent strengths of your Leadership Type, you can harness specific attributes that best align with the needs of the moment.

Equally important, your Leadership Type can help you identify gaps in your leadership capabilities—areas where you might benefit from adopting traits from another Leadership Type.

For instance, if you are a natural Visionary but struggle with the day-to-day operations of your team, you might incorporate traits from those who hold the power to structure, such as The Navigator or The Guide, to bolster your effectiveness in implementation. This awareness allows you to work on rounding out your skills, making you a more versatile leader.

In this final chapter, we leave you with some ideas of how to think bigger about what is possible, both for you as a leader and in terms of your impact on others when you take your understanding and knowledge of the Leadership Types into action.

Accelerate Self-Actualization

Self-actualization, a pinnacle in Maslow's hierarchy of needs, represents the realization of our full potential and the pursuit of personal growth, self-fulfillment, and self-awareness. Leadership Types play an instrumental role in facilitating this journey. By offering leaders a mirror to their intrinsic leadership styles, strengths, and vulnerabilities, Leadership Types allow for deep introspection. This heightened self-awareness not only sharpens a leader's understanding of their unique leadership blueprint but also illuminates pathways to hone their strengths and address areas of growth. When leaders operate from a place of self-awareness and authenticity, they are better positioned to pursue goals that are aligned with their core values and aspirations, propelling them closer to self-actualization.

Encourage Human Connection

The power of Leadership Types is not merely in their ability to categorize different styles of leaders but in their profound grounding in human motivation. By understanding their Leadership Types, leaders can tap into deep-seated motivations, both within themselves and those they lead. From a human psychology perspective, Leadership Types are an exploration of the psyche, delving into the intricate dance of desires, aspirations, and drivers that propel our actions. When leaders operate from this intrinsic space and deeper understanding of who they are and the impact they are seeking, the connection they establish with their teams can be more meaningful, organic, and transformative.

This is not about transactional leadership; it is about transformational experiences. The relationships built on the foundation of Leadership Types are resilient and empathetic, and they foster a shared vision through effectively bridging any gaps that might emerge from differing personalities or backgrounds. Harnessing the essence of their Leadership Types allows leaders to transcend mere role-based interactions, enabling them to communicate and cultivate relationships based on mutual understanding and respect. Recognizing and respecting the innate human motivations that drive each individual increases an overall sense of belonging, fosters inclusivity, and strengthens trust. When team members feel genuinely seen, valued, and understood at a core level, they are more likely to engage fully, contribute wholeheartedly, and invest emotionally in their roles. This heightened sense of belonging can dramatically increase team cohesion and pave the way for collaborative successes.

Additionally, the interconnected nature of Leadership Types aids in fostering interdepartmental and cross-functional connections. Understanding that a colleague operates from a certain motivational core allows for better communication, harmonized objectives, and the creation of a shared language. This mutual comprehension reduces the likelihood of conflicts and misunderstandings that often result from mismatched communication styles or differing leadership approaches. Instead of working in silos, departments can interlace their strategies, leveraging the strengths of each Leadership Type to create a holistic, cohesive organizational force.

But beyond organizational constructs, Leadership Types inspire leaders to connect on a human level. In a world increasingly dominated by technology and virtual interfaces, the thirst for genuine human connection is more profound than ever. By rooting leadership in core human motivations, Leadership Types offer pathways to authenticity in an often-impersonal, overly capitalistic, "winner takes all" corporate landscape. Leaders equipped with this understanding are more than efficient managers; they are agents for change who foster environments where human connections thrive, ideas flow freely, and collective visions come to life.

Set a Path for Building an Impactful Leadership Brand

Each Leadership Type encompasses a set of traits, values, strengths, and potential weaknesses that characterize the leader's approach and their unique manner of interaction with others within an organization. Just as **brand archetypes** allow companies to build a compelling brand identity, Leadership Types can enable leaders to develop a distinctive and coherent Leadership Brand identity.

Brand Archetypes

Quick Definition:

A brand archetype is a representation of a brand as a universally recognizable persona or role based on key human desires and values. Brand archetypes embody specific inherent traits, helping organizations to convey their values and mission through relatable narratives. These archetypes enable brands to establish a strong identity and differentiate themselves in competitive markets.

Three Key Things to Know About This Topic:
- Brand archetypes tap into the collective unconscious of and connect on a more emotional level with consumers, allowing companies to forge stronger and more meaningful connections with their audience.
- Utilizing archetypes in branding strategies helps in clearly defining a brand's personality, making it more memorable and appealing to the target audience.
- Archetypes guide the development of tailored marketing strategies that resonate deeply with consumers, enhancing consumer loyalty and brand advocacy.

Why You Should Care About This Topic As a Leader:

Organizations that embrace brand archetypes in their marketing and brand development efforts can better connect with customers or consumers and stand out in the marketplace. Archetypes not only help in crafting compelling narratives that resonate with audiences but also foster a consistent brand image that aligns with consumer expectations and emotions. By integrating these timeless symbols into your organization or product's brand strategy, you can drive deeper engagement, loyalty, and growth for your business.

To learn more about this topic,
visit leadershiptypes.com/resources/brand-archetypes/
or scan QR code:

When a company or organization creates a product or service brand that embodies an archetype, the implication is that the brand will be differentiated in the marketplace, gain market share, and increase value for the company or organization. When archetypes are active in a brand, that brand can connect with and evoke deep feelings in consumers and become most relevant to them. As Margaret Mark and Carol S. Pearson describe it in their book *The Hero and The Outlaw*, "Archetypal meaning is what makes brands come alive for people."[10]

Similarly, when an individual creates a Leadership Brand that clearly and consistently embodies a Leadership Type, the implication is that they will stand out with the potential to add even greater value or impact to the team, organization, or industry by connecting with, creating an emotional affinity with, and being more relevant to those around them. In the same way, Leadership Types can be a lever for change, influence, and impact.

Moreover, your Leadership Type can serve as a filter for your Leadership Brand's messaging and positioning. For instance, if you identify strongly with the power to awaken, your Leadership Brand could emphasize themes of innovation, courage, and disruptive change. You can reflect this branding in everything from your public speeches to your social media presence, ensuring that you attract opportunities, projects, and followers that resonate with your core motivation. Imagine crafting a LinkedIn profile or an About Me section on a corporate website that echoes these themes. You will naturally attract like-minded individuals and opportunities that align with your goals and values.

When a Leadership Brand is meticulously sculpted with a deep cognizance of Leadership Types, it becomes a vehicle for empowerment. And this is not just about visibility or recognition; it is about establishing a brand that acts as an accelerant to fuel a trajectory toward unwavering confidence, laser-focused clarity, and resonant impact. It is a brand narrative that does not just

---

10. Margaret Mark and Carol S. Pearson, *The Hero and the Outlaw: Building Extraordinary Brands Through the Power of Archetypes* (New York: McGraw Hill, 2001), 21.

echo titles or roles but amplifies a journey of barrier-breaking leadership.

The confluence of a person's inherent Leadership Type and their Leadership Brand is where magic unfolds. Rather than being just an aspirational image painted for the external world to see, it is a guiding star, a compass directing each decision and strategy with intentionality. This empowered branding is the touchstone in moments of ambiguity and challenge, offering not a retreat to the familiar but the audacity to chart unexplored terrains, anchored by the wisdom of their Leadership Type.

For those steering the helm of organizations, the imperative is profound: recognize the transformative potential embedded in the Leadership Type of every leader. By championing this brand-building odyssey, you strengthen the organizational fabric, revolutionizing its very essence. This is a commitment to a future in which leadership celebrates authenticity, embraces inclusivity, and achieves transformative resonance.

Promote More Effective Communication

Effective communication, the bedrock of impactful leadership, is significantly augmented by understanding and embracing our Leadership Types. Leaders equipped with insights into their distinctive style are more adept at modulating their communication to resonate with diverse audiences. Recognizing their Leadership Types means understanding their preferred modes of interaction, which allows them to tap into communication strategies that amplify their authentic voices while also attuning them to the needs and perceptions of their listeners. In essence, Leadership Types serve as a bridge that ensures the message transmitted by leaders is the message received by their teams, leading them to foster clarity, mutual understanding, and alignment.

When teams are introduced to the concept of Leadership Types, it opens avenues for enhanced interpersonal communication. By understanding the Leadership Types of their colleagues, team leaders can better predict, interpret, and respond to various communication styles. This mutual understanding reduces the scope for miscommunication, fosters empathy, and nurtures an environment in which diverse communication styles are respected and valued.

In a world where leadership landscapes are continuously evolving, the ability to communicate effectively is paramount. By offering leaders and teams a comprehensive framework, the SLE and its Leadership Types ensure that communication is not just about transmission but genuine connection. As leaders and teams navigate challenges, celebrate successes, and chart visions, the clarity and understanding brought about by Leadership Types ensure that the journey is collaborative, cohesive, and driven by mutual respect and understanding.

Serve as a Guide for Storytelling

Every leader carries a narrative, or a story of trials, triumphs, learnings, and legacies. Leadership Types serve as a guiding light in crystallizing and conveying this narrative with authenticity. With a clear understanding of their Leadership Types, leaders can weave stories that resonate, inspire, and influence.

The power of **storytelling in leadership** is unparalleled. Stories can drive change, inspire innovation, and foster loyalty. By using the framework of the SLE, leaders ensure that their stories are powerful tools of influence. Whether it is the narrative of a Catalyst challenging the status quo or a Champion upholding the values of an organization, understanding and leveraging Leadership Types adds depth, dimension, and direction to leadership storytelling.

Storytelling in Leadership

Quick Definition:

Storytelling in leadership is the strategic use of narrative to inspire, motivate, and convey values, transforming abstract concepts into relatable and actionable messages. It enables leaders to connect deeply with their audience, enhancing communication and fostering a strong organizational culture.

Three Key Things to Know About This Topic:
- Effective storytelling taps into emotions, making messages more memorable and impactful, which is crucial for motivating teams and driving organizational change.
- Storytelling helps embed organizational values and shape culture by illustrating these concepts through relatable narratives, making them more tangible and understandable.
- Leaders use storytelling as a tool to articulate vision, demonstrate values, and guide teams through complexities, making it an essential skill in effective leadership.

Why You Should Care About This Topic As a Leader:

Embracing storytelling as a leadership tool is vital because it significantly enhances your ability to communicate effectively and connect with your team on a deeper, more emotional level. Storytelling not only helps in aligning your team with the organizational goals by making them clear and compelling but also builds trust and loyalty, crucial for fostering a positive work environment and driving sustainable performance. As a leader, mastering storytelling can elevate your influence and effectiveness, enabling you to lead more dynamically and responsively in today's fast-paced world.

To learn more about this topic,
visit leadershiptypes.com/resources/storytelling-in-leadership/
or scan QR code:

Incorporating Leadership Types into storytelling also enables leaders to craft narratives that are both universal and deeply personal. While every Leadership Type speaks to a broader human experience and internal motivation, each also offers a unique lens through which individual stories can be tailored and told. For instance, a Visionary might recount a tale of foresight and innovation, while a Protector might share anecdotes of care, growth, and community. By aligning their stories with the underpinnings of their Leadership Types, both leaders can ensure that their narratives not only captivate but also evoke a deep sense of relatability and resonance with their audiences.

At its core, storytelling is about evoking emotion, imparting wisdom, and driving action. With Leadership Types serving as a foundation, leaders can seamlessly bridge the gap between their vision and their audience's perception. They can articulate challenges faced, solutions crafted, and visions realized in a manner that is aligned with their inherent leadership style. This consistency between who they are and the stories they tell amplifies their credibility and fosters trust. In an age when authenticity is prized, a narrative guided by a specific Leadership Type ensures that leaders are not just heard but also believed and followed.

Furthermore, storytelling driven by Leadership Types can become a cohesive force in creating diverse organizational landscapes where a myriad of voices, backgrounds, and perspectives intersect. By celebrating the diverse range of leadership styles and the unique stories each leader brings, organizations can foster a culture of inclusivity and mutual respect. Doing so encourages every leader, regardless of their Leadership Type, to embrace their unique journey and share it, thereby contributing to a richer, more multifaceted tapestry of collective organizational stories. It is about leading with intention and narrating with purpose, passion, and authenticity.

But telling your story is not just an act of self-expression; it is a crucial manifestation of your Leadership Brand. Your story provides a contextual framework that helps others understand who you are, what you stand for, and why you do what you do. It sets the stage for harnessing your authenticity, unique problem-solving approach, and the value you bring to the table. A compelling narrative does not just make you memorable; it creates emotional bonds that inspire loyalty, trust, and, ultimately, following. When people understand your journey, your challenges, and your triumphs, they are more likely to align with your vision and values, amplifying your influence as a leader.

Each Leadership Type serves as a lens through which you can craft and communicate your story resonantly. Understanding your Leadership Type can help you recognize key narrative elements that align with your core motivations and leadership style. For example, if you align with The Catalyst Leadership Type, you may weave into your story moments of pivotal change, risks taken, and paradigms challenged. This clarifies your understanding of your leadership journey and helps you articulate your story in a way that will resonate with like-minded individuals or those who aspire to similar forms of leadership.

Moreover, your Leadership Type can serve as a guide for the style, tone, and content of your storytelling. A leader driven by collaboration might tell their story in a way that emphasizes relationships, collaborative victories, and moments of empathy and understanding. This attracts those who share similar values and makes the story relatable on a human level, thereby expanding its reach and impact. Your Leadership Type becomes the narrative structure, the template that helps you organize your experiences into a coherent, compelling storyline that underscores your leadership identity.

In essence, your Leadership Type is more than just a category or label; it is a dynamic storytelling tool that helps you connect with others on a deep, psychological level. By aligning your story with your Leadership Type, you can create a cohesive Leadership Brand that is rooted in authenticity. It will be a brand that helps you differentiate yourself in a crowded leadership landscape and provides the emotional and intellectual hooks that draw people to you, keeping them engaged and inspiring them to act. Thus, the synergy between your story and your Leadership Type is more than effective branding; it is a pivotal element in the alchemy of leadership.

Enhance Networking, Relationship-Building, & Mentorship

Each Leadership Type naturally collaborates with some Types over others. Knowing your own can offer insights into why you click with certain individuals and how to foster effective partnerships. It can also guide you in mentorship, both in seeking mentors who can help you grow in targeted ways and in providing mentorship that plays to your strengths. Your Leadership Type thus becomes a continuous feedback tool, a way to iteratively refine your personal Leadership Brand for maximum impact and satisfaction.

Moreover, by promoting the understanding and acceptance of various Leadership Types, organizations can harness a powerful tool for mentorship and development. As emerging leaders are exposed to the richness of diverse leadership styles, they can find role models who resonate with their intrinsic strengths and aspirations. This is especially vital for individuals who might feel alienated or undervalued in their leadership journey due to patriarchal constructs. Through Leadership Types, they can see reflections of themselves in established leaders, deriving inspiration and gaining confidence in their unique leadership flair. This not only nurtures the next generation of diverse leaders but also dismantles patriarchal barriers that may have stifled their growth in the past.

Promote Effective Team Building

Leaders can proactively seek to build effective, complementary teams, ensuring a balance of Leadership Types that collectively drive organizational success. For example, in teams dealing with high-pressure projects or times of crisis, combining the resilience and drive of The Navigator with the optimism of The Pathfinder can ensure both steady progression and morale maintenance. Similarly, while The Trailblazer might constantly introduce new ideas and paradigms, The Connector can ensure that the entire team is on board, fostering unity and coherence amid the innovation.

Spark Organizational Transformation

Leadership Types catalyze organizational introspection and transformation. By adopting and promoting the SLE framework, organizations signal their commitment to challenging outdated leadership norms and making intentional strides toward diversity. This attracts a diverse pool of talent and bolsters the organization's image as a forward-thinking entity. External stakeholders, partners, and clients will recognize and appreciate the company's dedication to fostering a progressive leadership culture, aligning themselves with organizations that prioritize inclusivity. Over time, as increasingly more organizations embrace the tenets of Leadership Types, the corporate landscape will undergo a profound shift that will dismantle patriarchal relics and establish a new, inclusive standard for leadership.

Additionally, organizations can leverage the SLE to assess the composition of their leadership teams to ensure they have the necessary representation of the Leadership Types that may be required to drive organizational transformation. For example, an organization in stagnation that is seeking transformational growth through innovation will want to ensure adequate representation of leaders from quadrant 2 (the power to awaken), while an organization seeking to reorganize and stabilize after a crisis may look to ensure representation of more leaders from quadrant 4 (the power to structure).

Foster a Culture of Leadership

The application and implications of Leadership Types extend beyond the individual leader to help foster a culture of leadership throughout the organization. When members at all levels understand the concept of Leadership Types, they can identify their own leadership strengths and areas for growth. This promotes a culture in which everyone sees themselves as potential leaders regardless of their positions. The ripple effect is a more empowered, engaged, and proactive workforce, with individuals at all tiers feeling a sense of ownership and responsibility toward the collective vision and goals of the organization.

Create Your Legacy

Leadership is not merely a role; it is a profound expression of who we are. Every story shared and every Leadership Type explored has aimed to underscore one pivotal truth: authentic leadership emerges when we embrace our intrinsic narratives and motivations and harness them to forge meaningful connections.

The power of understanding your unique Leadership Type lies not just in self-awareness but in its cascading effects. When leaders align their actions and decisions with their inherent archetypical nature, they do not just function but thrive. They foster environments where teams feel understood, valued, and inspired. The ripples of such authentic leadership can transform organizational cultures, catalyze innovation, and pave the way for sustainable success through a shared vision.

However, recognizing your Leadership Type is just the beginning. The true journey commences when you apply this newfound knowledge in real-world scenarios, making choices that resonate with your Leadership Type. It is when you integrate these insights into daily leadership practices, from communication and decision-making to mentorship and innovation. It is about crafting a Leadership Brand that is built not on mimicry but on authenticity.

Embracing your Leadership Type is a commitment to leading with authenticity, purpose, and passion. It means acknowledging that your unique narrative has a place in the vast expanse of leadership styles and philosophies. It always has been. As you venture forward and harness the power of your Leadership Type, may you lead not just with authority but with confidence and heart, creating a legacy that stands the test of time.

When you turn the final page, know that this book serves as both an ending and a beginning. It is an ending to doubts, misdirection, and the idea that leadership comes from a mold you need to fit into. Most powerfully, it is the beginning of an era when your individuality will become your strongest leadership asset. For underrepresented leaders or those who have never seen themselves as leaders at all, this marks the start of a new chapter—one in which you are more than just part of the narrative; you are the author of it. Our focus on diversity, *empowerment*, and inclusion is a declaration that leadership has room for *all* voices, especially those who have been marginalized or hushed. This is your platform and your moment to step into your leadership destiny.

Through celebrating the multiplicity of leadership styles and attempting to dismantle long-held leadership stereotypes, the SLE allows us to acknowledge and applaud the fact that leadership comes in various forms and styles. Recognizing and appreciating these variations is pivotal in today's globalized world because it allows organizations to be more inclusive by harnessing diverse leadership styles to navigate their multifaceted challenges. The SLE is thus an evolutionary step in the realm of leadership development. It provides a nuanced, tailored, and dynamic approach to understanding and practicing leadership. By grounding leaders in their authentic strengths while allowing them flexibility to adapt and evolve, Leadership Types set the stage for genuine, impactful, and resonant leadership in the modern world. As leaders continue to shape and define their paths, having the SLE as a compass can prove invaluable, ensuring a journey that is both meaningful and effective.

So, what is your next step? The SLE is not a static model but a dynamic, evolving guide, reflective of your own growth and the complexities of the challenges you will encounter. Keep it at hand as a tool for ongoing self-assessment, a barometer for interpersonal dynamics, and a playbook for strategic decision-making. As you evolve, so will your understanding of your Leadership Type and its application. Revisit this knowledge often, share it with your teams, mentor aspiring leaders, and use it as a cornerstone for establishing your own leadership academies or training programs.

Remember, the pursuit of authentic leadership is a journey without a final destination. It is an ongoing commitment to greatness—not just for you but for the communities and organizations you impact. Here's to your BREAKTHRU and to the incredible journey that lies ahead.

ACKNOWLEDGMENTS

I would like to start by thanking my wife, Lindsay Gaskins, for encouraging me to start BREAKTHRU Brands in the first place, and for lovingly pushing me to become an author. More importantly, thank you for helping me be brave and step into my own identity over two decades ago. Thank you for your integrity as a person and your unwavering love and support, both as my wife and as a mother to our three amazing daughters. And thank you for reminding me to find joy, that it is okay if things are a little messy and not perfect, and for pushing us to make bold plans. Together we can do anything.

Thank you to my parents, who helped me set a foundation of self-esteem, self-worth, and self-assurance required to become a leader. Thanks to them, I now have the audacity to speak out and write about leadership empowerment.

To my dad, Ross Barnard, who has read every leadership book under the sun and has shared his wisdom and insights with me in small and large ways since before I could even walk or talk. Thank you for teaching me how to lead.

To my mom, Linda Barnard, who has always been the perfect Navigator and Protector for our family. Thank you for being there for us and for showing me what leading with love in your heart looks like.

To Kathy Delaney-Smith, who not only coached me on the basketball court but also prepared me to lead authentically and served as the inspiration for our business from day one. Thank you for giving me the courage and confidence to take all the leaps in life.

Finally, this book would not have come to life without the collaboration, creative ideas, diligent research, and hard work of our team at BREAKTHRU, in particular our brilliant partner and chief strategist, Hallie Robinson, and our diligent researcher and copywriter, Katherine Yocum. Thank you to the empathetic, highly skilled, and dynamic duo of Lorrie Cardwell-Panfil and LaTasha Brown, who lead the insights-gathering and storytelling for our impact-driven clients at BREAKTHRU. It has been so amazing to see all of this come together in the SLE and throughout the pages of this book. Lindsay and I are extremely grateful for you all and for the opportunity to empower a wider audience of leaders with our approach.

BIBLIOGRAPHY

Armstrong, Martin. "It Will Take Another 136 Years to Close the Global Gender Gap." World Economic Forum. April 12, 2021. https://www.weforum.org/agenda/2021/04/136-years-is-the-estimated-journey-time-to-gender-equality/.

Fry, Richard. "Women Now Outnumber Men in the U.S. College-Educated Labor Force." Pew Research Center. September 26, 2022. https://www.pewresearch.org/short-reads/2022/09/26/women-now-outnumber-men-in-the-u-s-college-educated-labor-force/.

Harkema, Graci. "How to Bring Your Authentic Self to Work." Ascend. December 15, 2023. https://hbr.org/2023/12/how-to-bring-your-authentic-self-to-work.

Mark, Margaret and Carol S. Pearson, *The Hero and the Outlaw: Building Extraordinary Brands Through the Power of Archetypes*. New York: McGraw Hill, 2001.

Milad, Michael. "Female Leadership: Overcoming Stereotypes about Choosing the Best Leader." *Forbes*. January 26, 2021. https://www.forbes.com/sites/forbescoachescouncil/2021/01/26/female-leadership-overcoming-stereotypes-about-choosing-the-best-leader/?sh=2f24e9051ccb.

Minkin, Rachel. "Diversity, Equity and Inclusion in the Workplace." Pew Research Center. May 17, 2023. https://www.pewresearch.org/social-trends/2023/05/17/diversity-equity-and-inclusion-in-the-workplace/.

Nguyễn, Ann Thúy, and Maya Pendleton. "Recognizing Race in Language: Why We Capitalize 'Black' and 'White.'" Center for the Study of Social Policy. March 23, 2020. https://cssp.org/2020/03/recognizing-race-in-language-why-we-capitalize-black-and-white/.

Vespa, Jonathan, Lauren Medina, and David M. Armstrong. "Demographic Turning Points for the United States: Population Projections for 2020 to 2060." United States Census Bureau. Last modified February 2020. https://www.census.gov/content/dam/Census/library/publications/2020/demo/p25-1144.pdf.

Villarreal, Alexandra. "White Male Minority Rule Pervades Politics across the US, Research Shows." *The Guardian*. May 26, 2021. https://www.theguardian.com/us-news/2021/may/26/white-male-minority-rule-us-politics-research.

Yuan, Lily. "Guide: 12 Jungian Archetypes as Popularized by the Hero and the Outlaw." Personality Psychology. January 3, 2022. https://personality-psychology.com/guide-12-jungian-archetypes/.

ABOUT THE AUTHOR

LAURA BARNARD
FOUNDER | BEHAVIORAL MARKETING EXPERT | SPEAKER | AUTHOR

Laura Barnard, The Visionary founder of BREAKTHRU Brands, embarked on a mission to transform the landscape of leadership. With a philosophy rooted in breaking barriers and championing equity, Barnard leverages her extensive experience in leading global brands to build a future where diverse voices in leadership are not just heard but celebrated and amplified.

Barnard's journey, influenced by her academic pursuits in psychology at Harvard University and an MBA in marketing and strategic management from the University of Chicago Booth School of Business, reflects a deep understanding of the intersection between brand power and leadership dynamics.

As a former Division I athlete and a current proud member of the LGBTQIA+ community, Barnard infuses her work with energy, collaboration, and a relentless drive for inclusivity. Her approach is not just about developing leaders; it is about nurturing authentic and bold leaders to shape a more equitable world.

Barnard resides in Oak Park, Illinois, with her wife, Lindsay Gaskins, and their three daughters.

THE B CORP MOVEMENT

Dear reader,

Thank you for reading this book and joining the Publish Your Purpose community! You are joining a special group of people who aim to make the world a better place.

What's Publish Your Purpose About?

Our mission is to elevate the voices often excluded from traditional publishing. We intentionally seek out authors and storytellers with diverse backgrounds, life experiences, and unique perspectives to publish books that will make an impact in the world. Beyond our books, we are focused on tangible, action-based change. As a woman- and LGBTQ+-owned company, we are committed to reducing inequality, lowering levels of poverty, creating a healthier environment, building stronger communities, and creating high-quality jobs with dignity and purpose.

As a Certified B Corporation, we use business as a force for good. We join a community of mission-driven companies building a more equitable, inclusive, and sustainable global economy. B Corporations must meet high standards of transparency, social and environmental performance, and accountability as determined by the nonprofit B Lab. The certification process is rigorous and ongoing (with a recertification requirement every three years).

How Do We Do This?

We intentionally partner with socially and economically disadvantaged businesses that meet our sustainability goals. We embrace and encourage our authors and employee's differences in race, age, color, disability, ethnicity, family or marital status, gender identity or expression, language, national origin, physical and mental ability, political affiliation, religion, sexual orientation, socio-economic status, veteran status, and other characteristics that make them unique.

Community is at the heart of everything we do—from our writing and publishing programs to contributing to social enterprise nonprofits like reSET (www.resetco.org) and our work in founding B Local Connecticut.

We are endlessly grateful to our authors, readers, and local community for being the driving force behind the equitable and sustainable world we are building together.

To connect with us online, or publish with us, visit us at www.publishyourpurpose.com.

Elevating Your Voice,

Jenn T Grace

Jenn T. Grace
Founder, Publish Your Purpose